Technology,
Entrepreneurs,
and
Silicon Valley

Stanford University, 1906. After the earthquake.

Technology,
Entrepreneurs,
and
Silicon Valley

*In memory of our good friend and
brilliant writer Ward Winslow*

1927—2000

Publisher: John McLaughlin
Authors: Carol Whiteley
John McLaughlin
Project Manager: Gina Woolf
Art Director: Keith Costas
Photo Editor/Archivist: Sally McBurney

First Edition

Library of Congress Catalog Card Number: 2001096087
Whiteley, Carol 1946–
McLaughlin, John, 1949–
ISBN 0-9649217-1-5

Published in Palo Alto, California, USA
Printed in China

CONTENTS

Almost 10 years ago the Santa Clara Valley Historical Association began to record the stories of the individuals who created the greatest technological revolution in history. Because of these people, the world has changed. In our first book, *The Making of Silicon Valley: A 100 Year Renaissance*, we compared the contributions of Silicon Valley as equal to or greater than those of the Italian Renaissance of Leonardo da Vinci and Michelangelo.

Our mission, from the beginning, has been to interview world-impacting individuals as though we were asking questions 500 years from now. What would future historians want to know?

The important questions have been about mentors, discoveries, luck, and failure. Our subjects have been more than open; we have always ended each session enlightened. The very first interview was with the late Linus Pauling, twice the recipient of the Nobel Prize. Soon afterwards we interviewed the late Bill Hewlett and the late Dave Packard. To date, the Association has conducted and filmed over 130 interviews. Quotes from these interviews are interspersed throughout this book.

Luck is often as important an ingredient as determination in our work. Both factors played an important part in recruiting Walter Cronkite to narrate our first documentary, which aired nationwide on PBS. Silicon Valley's story is an extraordinary one, and we were determined to tell it with the voices of many who participated in it.

During our endeavor to accomplish what the Association considered a worthy task, we encountered many of the same obstacles that high-technology entrepreneurs deal with: rising rents, funding problems, employees with self-enriching agendas, copyright litigation (the Association was the plaintiff), competitors with identical plans (they disappeared), and, finally, the loss of one of our key members—Ward Winslow.

I can't say enough good things about Ward Winslow. He was a great writer, honest, witty, a gentleman to a fault, and a beloved friend to all of us. This book is dedicated to his memory.

In our struggle to replace Ward Winslow's talent and contributions we found an inner strength. Ward had already set the standard for us to follow. Our core group, which consists of Gina Woolf, Sally McBurney, Keith Costas and myself, has been with the Association for more than eight years. A new professional writer has joined the team: Carol Whiteley.

There are other individuals whose kindness and optimism have been an invaluable source of support. We thank them with all our hearts. Two organizations that have always provided us with advice and made their resources accessible are the Palo Alto Historical Association and Stanford University.

During the last 10 years I have experienced more incredible moments of discovery and understanding than I could have received while obtaining 20 college degrees. It's one thing to study Christopher Columbus—all of the important dates and discoveries—but it would be an entirely different fountain of knowledge to interview Columbus. You could ask where he got his ideas, who his mentors were, if he got lucky when he discovered America, how many times he failed in life, why he chose to take such great risks.

When I interviewed Hewlett, Packard, Jobs, Woz, Bushnell, Clark, McNealy, Engelbart, and dozens of others, I always asked the questions that I believe any historian would love to ask Christopher Columbus.

I wouldn't trade my job for all the tea in China.

For those of you who live in Silicon Valley, there are always trade-offs. On the positive side, you're on the cutting edge of technology, though there's no way you can understand and be on top of it all. On the negative side, it's too crowded and things cost too much. The cost of a home is astronomical by any standard.

Here are a couple of stories that might make you feel better:

Before the printing of the Association's first book, I flew to Singapore to select a good printer. During a tour of the Toppan Printing plant, a group of managers escorted me into a conference room and pretended to be interested in my project. I offered to play for them a five-minute videotape that had a sampling of the personalities who had contributed their knowledge to the book and upcoming documentary. Being polite, the Toppan group studiously watched the video. Images of Hewlett, Woz, and Jobs filled the screen. The video ended. All heads turned towards me, mouths open.

I asked, "Is something wrong?"

The General Manager spoke up: "All of us took a tour of Silicon Valley last month. We visited Intel, HP, Silicon Graphics, and Varian before going to University Avenue in Palo Alto to wait for him."

"For who?" I asked.

"Steve Jobs! He never came. We waited in the Good Earth Restaurant for two hours and he never showed up to eat his lunch!" one man replied.

I smiled as I imagined most of the tables at the Good Earth filled with several dozen hopeful Jobs groupies.

Once *The Making of Silicon Valley: A 100 Year Renaissance* was published, it became a local bestseller. Many Silicon Valley companies kept ordering additional books to replace those "borrowed" from their reception areas.

Late one fall afternoon, a man with a distinctive Indian accent telephoned the Association from a company in Fremont. He wanted to come to the office and purchase a copy of *The Making of Silicon Valley: A 100 Year Renaissance*.

When he appeared, he told me that he needed the book because Bangalore, India, was going to be the next Silicon Valley. He wanted to use the book to track how much faster it was happening in India.

The man proudly said, "I have $30 million invested in my company. We have government support, great relations with the universities, the pick of the best minds from the Indian universities. Tell me why Bangalore won't become bigger than Silicon Valley!"

I replied, "What if something unforeseen happens and, despite your best efforts, your company goes broke? What happens to you?"

"I would have to leave India!" he said. "I couldn't stay there if I failed."

Because I had heard so many stories about risk and failure from so many Silicon Valley pioneers, I had to reply, "Unless you change India's attitude towards failure, Bangalore and most other high-tech areas in the world will not duplicate the growth and success of Silicon Valley."

In business, as in other parts of life, failure is commonplace. If an athlete drops the ball, he gets up and learns from his error. When a scientist fails at an experiment, he tries again, a different way. In Silicon Valley, when entrepreneurs attempt a new business concept and fail, they learn from the experiment and try again. Nowhere else in the world is failure so accepted as a tool for success. Fraud is not acceptable—you'd better be honest and forthright—but failure is acceptable, and part of the making of Silicon Valley.

Silicon Valley and the San Francisco Bay Area comprise one of the most forgiving and tolerant cradles of civilization in the world. Ethnic, religious, and racial diversity are the norm. Streets, towns, and cities are filled with Caucasians of European descent, Mexican families, Jewish and Catholic families, African-American families, Asian families, Middle Eastern families, people from every corner and every religion in the world.

As the Santa Clara Valley Historical Association enters a new decade, we've decided to use our roots to both broaden and narrow our scope. Invention and advances in technology take place all over the world, and we want to be able to record these innovations wherever they occur. Too often, however, the Santa Clara Valley Historical Association has been associated with plumes and prunes from the diminishing orchards that once graced the commercial landscape. So we've changed our name to the Institute for the History of Technology. We've already come a long way. We hope that we can contribute even more.

John R. McLaughlin
Founder and President
Institute for the History of Technology
john@historytech.org

Acknowledgments

The Institute for the History of Technology would like to thank the following companies for their generous support as Premier Sponsors:

Avaya
IBM Corporation
Inktomi Corporation
Intel Corporation
NEC Electronics, Inc.
Varian Medical Systems

We would also like to give special thanks to the following companies for their support: Acuson Corporation, Adaptec Inc., Adobe Systems, Agilent Technologies, Alain Pinel Realtors, AOL/Netscape, Apple, Asyst Technologies, Atmel Corporation, Autodesk, Bank of America, Cisco Systems, Coherent, Inc., Cypress Semiconductor, Flextronics International Ltd., Fujitsu Software Corporation, Hewlett-Packard Company, Hitachi, Ltd., Infineon Technologies, Keeble and Shuchat, Linear Technology, Mentor Graphics Corporation, Network Appliance, Oracle Corporation, Pacific Maintenance, Philips Semiconductors, PricewaterhouseCoopers LLP, Quantum Corporation, Samsung Semiconductor, Siemens AG, SONICblue, Sound Advantage LLC, SRI International, Therma, Inc., Toeniskoetter & Breeding, Inc., Trend Micro, Inc., Tyco Electronics Corporation, Vishay Intertechnology, Inc., and Wilson Sonsini Goodrich & Rosati.

The Palo Alto Historical Association and Stanford University were important sources of historical photographs and information. We gratefully acknowledge their assistance.

Thanks also go to the following individuals for their support:
Charles Atthill, Keith Costas, James Gibbons, Craig Johnson, Erin Kingston-Costas, Alice Kleeman, Les Laky, Sally McBurney, Helene Scott, Gary Simpson, Murray Suid, Carol Whiteley, Paul Wilcox, Susan Bright Winn, Holly Winslow, David Wong, Bill Woolf, and Gina Woolf.

In addition to their support of the publication of this book, the sponsoring corporations and firms, in keeping with the educational and cultural objectives of The Institute for the History of Technology, are distributing copies of this book to the high schools, colleges, and universities of their choice.

WORLD-CLASS COMPONENTS: THE POWER BEHIND THE PRODUCTS

While the advent of the computer revolutionized our ability to communicate and learn, the components that power the computer have undergone several revolutions themselves. Twenty-first-century computing devices are now undergoing their fifth transformation, housing components unimaginable when the earliest electronic computer was first conceptualized.

Thomas Edison, who is well remembered as an inventor, also made an extremely important scientific discovery that eventually affected the computer. Edison found that electricity will travel through space from a heated metal, a phenomenon he dubbed the Edison effect. When the electron was discovered by J. J. Thomson in 1897, the Edison effect was explained as electrons boiling off metal. It was later determined that electrons travel only to a positively charged terminal, and that, since alternating current switches back and forth from positive to negative, the Edison effect could be used to turn alternating current into direct current. This was a great advance for electrical equipment such as radio receivers, which would not work with alternating current.

A device that was developed by Sir John Ambrose Fleming that turned alternating current into direct current became known as a rectifier, and was found to be most effective in a vacuum. The first rectifiers were enclosed in partially evacuated glass tubes and greatly improved the workings of the radio, which had previously relied on crystals for rectification. But tubes, or valves, as they were called in England, did not depend only on the flow of electricity; they also depended on the control of electrons. Tubes, therefore, became known as electronic, rather than electrical.

But while tubes made possible effective radios and televisions, they had numerous operational problems: after continual heating, their metal eventually boiled away and the vacuum degraded. In addition, the power needed for the Edison effect was high and caused heat buildup, and the tubes themselves were fairly large. When the first digital computers were constructed, toward the end of World War II, they housed tubes to rectify the current. But they needed

> *"The first enterprise here was the old Mackay Radio. And that was started by a guy named Cyril Elwell. He started this company, bought the patents, came back and raised the capital while he was here. And it's interesting that David Starr Jordan encouraged some of his faculty to buy some of this stock. So you might say that he was the first venture capitalist."*
>
> —Bill Hewlett, Founder of Hewlett-Packard

Mackay Radio

Shockley's Traitorous Eight: In 1957, these young men quit Shockley Semiconductor to found Fairchild Semiconductor, a move that would change the world forever.

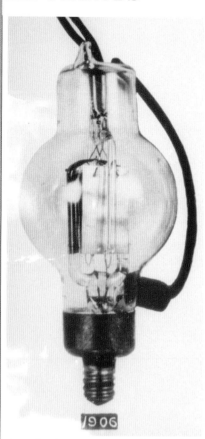

Lee de Forest's "queer little tube." Although the subject of a criminal indictment alleging fraud, this queer little tube enabled transatlantic radio transmission for the first time.

so many tubes—one computer, the ENIAC, had 18,000—that powering them often caused the lights to dim, and they failed frequently. The sizable tube-filled computers also produced an enormous amount of heat that had to be dissipated.

Because of these and other problems, scientists began to look into new types of rectifiers. At Bell Telephone Laboratories, William Shockley, working with John Bardeen and Walter Brattain, found that impure crystals of germanium, a different type of crystal than had been previously used to rectify current, could be modified to produce crystals that were as good rectifiers as tubes. These crystals, with attached wire contacts, were also able to amplify current. Shockley and his fellow scientists called the crystals transistors.

Transistors turned out to have none of the problems of tubes. They were small, didn't require a vacuum, were longer lasting and more reliable, and produced much less heat. And because they were so tiny, more than one could fit on a piece of crystal, or chip, as these slivers of crystal later became called.

By the mid-fifties, many companies were producing different types of transistors. Then, in 1957, a technique invented by Jean Hoerni revolutionized the way transistors were made. Using Hoerni's "planar technique," and crystals of silicon rather than germanium, transistors were developed using a series of processes. First, a slice, or wafer,

of silicon was oxidized. Then it was coated with a photosensitive material called a photoresist. Next, a pattern was photographed on the resist, which became vulnerable to certain chemicals when placed in light. The pattern was etched through the resist as well as the oxide. Finally, the resist was washed off and the impurities allowed to spread onto the exposed parts of the wafer. The rest of the wafer was protected by the remaining oxide. All of these processes were repeated to form numerous conducting layers.

Transistors made with the planar technique were immediately put to use in radios, hearing aids, TVs, and computers. They also encouraged engineers to design more complex electron circuits that contained hundreds or thousands of discrete components, including transistors, rectifiers, diodes, and capacitors. Increasingly powerful circuits were produced, but all of the many components had to be soldered by hand to tiny pieces of wire. Researchers were challenged to find a less expensive, less time consuming way to produce and interconnect them.

At Texas Instruments, in 1958, Jack Kilby began to work on the problem. Instead of taking his traditional two-week vacation, he turned his inventive mind to looking for an alternative way to provide the electronic circuits that had recently become known as semiconductors. He determined that resistors and capacitors, the passive devices, could be made from the same material—germanian—as the transistors, or active devices. And because of that

> When we first made transistors at Fairchild, we sold them for $150 a piece. When they went into volume production they were $5 or $10 a piece. Now you can buy yourself an integrated circuit with millions of transistors on it. And the cost has gone down over a million fold. And you get the circuit design and everything for nothing. This effect could never have been imagined when we got started at Fairchild.
>
> **Gordon Moore, Founder of Fairchild Semiconductor**

> You try very hard to predict what is going to happen in your environment, and then start to build the capability to take advantage of that environment today. If you don't start until it's there, you can be eclipsed by a competitor. So we try to focus a little bit out—about a year—but, frankly, every three months you have to take stock of where you are, what the marketplace is telling you, what your customers are telling you, what your competitors are doing. You have to make sure that you've got your resource allocation done correctly, that you're doing the smart things to balance the long term for the short term.
>
> **Meg Whitman, CEO of eBay**

they could all be made as one, incorporated onto a single chip. A few months after his breakthrough, Kilby demonstrated a working integrated circuit built on one semiconductor.

At about the same time, Robert Noyce and a number of chemists, researchers, engineers, and metallurgists started up a company funded by Fairchild Camera and Instrument—a company that became Fairchild Semiconductor. There the team, led by Noyce, created the first commercially viable integrated circuit, the device that is credited with creating the modern computer industry. For their work in developing the integrated circuit, Robert Noyce and Jack Kilby were later awarded the Nobel Prize.

In the sixties, the use of integrated circuits in computers began to take off,

arly Intel silicon wafer
chnology and the invention
f the microprocessor paved
e way for the personal
mputer and, later, the
ternet.

Dr. William Shockley, Nobel Laureate for his work on the transistor. He once commented that the transistor would have been invented sooner had World War II not diverted his energies.

I t's curious that both millennium celebrations, 1000 AD and 2000 AD, resulted in great awakenings: the first in spiritual values and the second in shareholder values.

Les Laky, Investor

replacing the circuits made up of separate discrete components. Integrated circuits became increasingly sophisticated as more and more components were packed onto a chip, and the price of an IC dropped to $1. But though ICs became cheaper and more powerful, they still could perform only limited tasks and in limited ways. They had to be soldered into a rigid pattern on a printed circuit board, which actually made them less flexible than the tube-filled computers of the '40s.

At Intel Corporation, an engineer named Marcian "Ted" Hoff developed a way to put a computer's entire central processing capabilities on a single chip. This chip became known as a microprocessor, and could react in fixed ways like an IC but also could have its response altered. Coupling the microprocessor with other Intel innovations—the RAM (random access memory) chip, which can read memory cells at will, and the ROM (read-only memory) chip, whose information can't be altered—enabled computers to run faster, perform many more tasks, and take up much less space. Ted Hoff's invention of the microprocessor led to the revolutionary age of the microcomputer.

Since the first circuit was constructed on a chip, circuit elements have continued to grow progressively smaller, so that now more than a million circuits can be packed onto one tiny chip. Even entire systems can be housed on one chip. Such miniaturization has enabled faster device performance times, less heat buildup, less energy consumption, and lower costs. It has also encouraged the design of specialized chips, including CCD (charge-coupled device), or imager, chips, which can detect the tiniest flaws, even in other chips; and flash EPROM (erasable programmable read-only memory), which can be erased and reprogrammed at very high speeds, among many other chip innovations. As they have been for many years, circuit designers are currently at work creating the ICs of the future that will once again revolutionize our electronic devices and greatly increase our capabilities.

T he creative person embraces the paradox of forsaking the known for the prospect of emptiness. New discoveries emerge when the comfort of predictability stimulates the adventurous to leap into the void of possibility. Over time, the successful push forward, casting about for a new edge from which to survey vistas of an unimaginable landscape of opportunity. Creative people leap off cliffs. They don't see danger. Instead, they imagine a landscape of opportunity. And they find it.

Jo Ellen Eng, Chairperson of the Brooks Institute of Photography

MIPS Technologies made history in 1985 with its R4000, the first true 64-bit commercial RISC processor.

1GB DIMM (RAM) (photo courtesy of Infineon Technologies)

Philo Farnsworth

As a 14-year-old boy working on his family's Idaho potato field, Philo Farnsworth had a vision that images could be transmitted electronically. By age 21, in 1927, Farnsworth had built the first working model of a television at his laboratory in San Francisco.

Vladimir Zworykin, a Russian émigré, had made a patent application for television in 1923, but didn't produce a working model until 1931. By 1931, Zworykin was working with the Radio Corporation of America (RCA). RCA had no intention of recognizing Farnsworth's invention or paying him royalties. "RCA doesn't pay royalties," RCA president David Sarnoff said, "we collect them."

After many years of litigation and appeals, RCA agreed to begin paying Farnsworth royalties on the license of his television invention. But the patent rights soon expired and Farnsworth received little money.

Philo Farnsworth passed away in 1971.

Philo Farnsworth in his San Francisco workshop, circa 1928

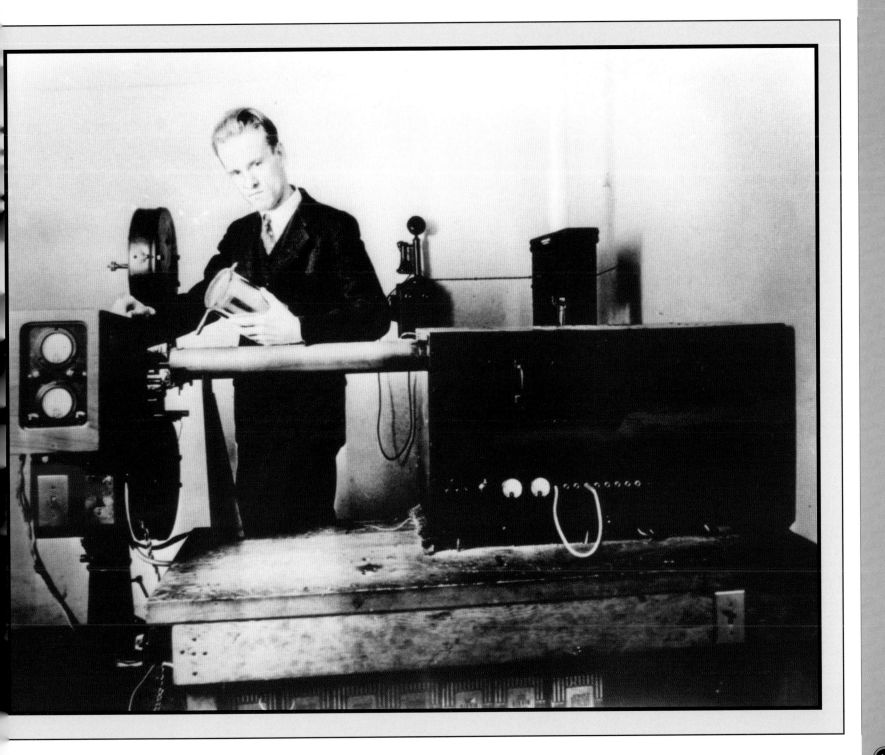

NEC ELECTRONICS INC.

www.necel.com

In 1999, NEC Electronics' parent company, NEC Corporation, celebrated its 100th year in business by making a fundamental change in company direction for its next 100 years. While it traditionally had been a hardware provider, manufacturing a wide array of top-performing semiconductors, communications equipment, and computers, NEC Corporation chose to center its product focus on the Internet and become an organization that could help its customers find complete solutions in our Internet-driven world.

NEC Electronics is playing a major role in advancing that new mission. While NEC Corporation was founded as a joint venture with Western Electric Company in Japan, and has an enormous presence there, NEC Electronics has been an important part of Silicon Valley since the company was founded in Santa Clara in 1981. Established to consolidate the production and marketing of NEC's expanding array of semiconductors, NEC Electronics, headed by president and CEO Hirokazu Hashimoto, is now one of the leading semiconductor manufacturers in the United States. The company's manufacturing facility, which opened in Roseville, California, in 1984, is one of the largest semiconductor fabrication facilities in the world.

When NEC Corporation announced its new direction, it also announced a realignment of its operations into three in-house companies: NEC

Mr. Hirokazu Hashimoto, president and CEO, NEC Electronics Inc.

Solutions, NEC Networks, and NEC Electron Devices. Each company provides complete design, development, manufacturing, and sales capabilities, and together provide the platform that has launched NEC into the burgeoning Internet market. NEC Solutions delivers a broad spectrum of e-commerce and Internet solutions, including systems integration and networking services. NEC Networks provides crucial networking assistance to network service providers, and NEC Electron Devices advances the equipment that makes the Internet work. Together with NEC Electron Devices, NEC Electronics develops and manufactures the electronic components that power Internet equipment.

NEC Electronics has the capability of offering standard products, application-specific products (products developed for one type of application, such as set-top boxes), and a path to complete system integration. System integration combines specific hardware with application software and peripherals and houses them all on a single chip. This "system on chip," or SOC, device takes the place of several individual chips, enabling smaller and more powerful end products.

NEC Electronics is a premier supplier of microcontrollers, microprocessors, and network controllers. Its K Series® microcontrollers operate within an extended range of temperatures, enable power management features, and are ideal for office products, cellular phones, and two-way pagers. The K Series and the V800® Series microcontrollers are also powerful in automotive applications such as audio electronics. The company's network controllers provide a versatile and cost-effective way to bring broadband (high-speed communication over a long distance) access to small businesses and home offices.

In the world of complex electronic component design, NEC Electronics has the resources and the expertise to take customers from concept to a working silicon product. The company has a proven array of devices for high-performance, low-power applications, plus the technology to enable the integration of more than a hundred million 0.13-micron transistors on a single chip. To reduce product development time, their OpenCAD® design system combines proprietary design tools with widely used electronic

NEC's 42" plasma display features high brightness and low power consumption.

design automation tools and deep submicron, or "design miniaturation," technology.

NEC Electronics also provides innovative solutions for diverse consumer products. Their encoders expand the features of set-top boxes, and their liquid crystal display (LCD) drivers improve the quality of cellular phone and personal digital assistant displays. Their flat-panel displays produce bright, high-contrast images, and their rechargeable, lightweight lithium-ion batteries can be used in a wide range of climates and extend the operating time of portable and wireless devices.

Some of NEC Electronics' sophisticated semiconductors are produced at the company's Roseville manufacturing site. Using the most advanced manufacturing equipment and technologies, including a state-of-the-art robotics system, the facility produces more than 50,000 wafers a month. Round-the-clock production cycles keep up with the demand for the latest in semiconductor technology, plus

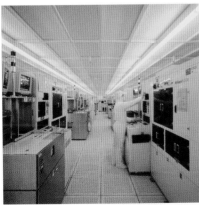

NEC's Roseville, California, semiconductor manufacturing plant

NEC's network controller is powered by a high-performance 100 MHz MIPS CPU host processor VR4130™ and combines best-of-breed solutions from IteX™ and WindRiver®. It is the ideal reference design to meet the emerging requirements of wired ADSL applications.

process and product engineers are always available to work with customers to get products to market faster. To help keep their community clean and safe, engineers have implemented innovative techniques that have allowed the plant to decrease off-site hazardous-waste disposal by more than 60%. In addition, recycling programs enable the reuse of enough water each year to fill 12,000 swimming pools and save 4,000 trees. Six hundred thousand square feet of space are currently being added to the plant to house the production of system-on-chip devices as well as other advanced devices.

In addition to its Roseville site and its Santa Clara headquarters, NEC Electronics has 20 regional sales offices and seven design and technical centers serving clients throughout the United States. At all of its locations, the company works to support the local communities by encouraging employee volunteerism and contributing to hundreds of organizations that promote the arts, education, youth enrichment, and health and human services. For example, NEC Electronics supports the efforts of InnVision, a program that provides emergency shelter and long-term housing for the homeless in Santa

Clara County. The company also awards REACH scholarships to high school seniors who have overcome adversity and sponsors a Corporate Volunteer Commitment Program that gives many hours of time to special community projects.

With an inventory of over 5,000 products suitable for applications, including hubs and routers, handheld PCs, notebook PCs, workstations, personal digital assistants, and safety systems, NEC Electronics can offer complete solutions to businesses designing next-generation computing and Internet products. And with the expertise of its own design, production, and technical departments, plus the backing of the global manufacturing capabilities and multi-billion-dollar resources of parent NEC Corporation, NEC Electronics can enable customers to have shorter design cycles, a secure component supply, and a faster time to market.

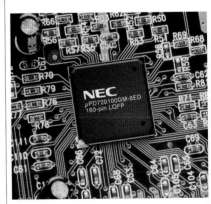

NEC leads in USB 2.0 (Universal Serial Bus) development. USB provides a universal plug-and-play solution between a wide variety of PCs and PC peripherals.

SAMSUNG SEMICONDUCTOR

www.usa.samsungsemi.com

Samsung Semiconductor, Inc., headquartered in San Jose, California, is a wholly owned subsidiary of Korea-based Samsung Electronics. Headed by President Han Joo Kim, Samsung Semiconductor leads the North American marketing efforts for the sophisticated semiconductor components that Samsung manufactures—components that are used by the world's leading computer, multimedia, home appliance, information, and telecommunications producers. Samsung uses a combination of distribution channels and OEM sales to serve its customer base and maintains a large network of sales representatives and distributors throughout North America.

Samsung is the world's fourth largest semiconductor supplier overall and the number two supplier in North America. Samsung is also the world's memory market leader in both DRAM and SRAM. Its broad range of products includes all types of memory, ASIC, microcontrollers, multimedia devices, and TFT-LCD displays.

As a technology innovator and leader, Samsung is focused on providing its customers with state-of-the-art solutions. A long record of industry firsts, the most recent being the realization in silicon of the world's first 4Gb DRAM, illustrates the company's unwavering commitment to this goal.

Samsung's steady commitment to technology, quality, and service is the

"We at Samsung Semiconductor are committed to our leadership role in providing our customers with state-of-the-art semiconductor products right here in Silicon Valley."
–Han Joo Kim, President

cornerstone of its success. Strict adherence to guidelines for quality assurance has earned the company the International Standards Organization's highest rating for quality: ISO9000.

In the year 2000, Samsung invested more than nine percent of its total revenue in R&D, a figure greater than most of the other leading electronics companies. The company's semiconductor operations include 12 advanced R&D and manufacturing centers. Its research and development efforts and high-volume production are performed in the company's own facilities in Kiheung, Onyang, and Chonan in Korea; and in the United States, in Austin, Texas.

Samsung is the world's largest supplier of DRAM products, with a comprehensive product offering that includes RDRAM, DDR (Double-Data-Rate) SDRAM, and SDRAM, all in a full range of speeds and densities. In addition to discrete components, Samsung also offers a complete line of modules, up to 1-Gbyte DIMM, and has given top priority to expanding its product offering to meet future customers' system requirements. With DDR SDRAM and RDRAM, Samsung continues to be the leader in meeting next-generation system requirements.

Samsung is also one of the world's largest suppliers of graphics memory products and has the widest product range. Current flagship products include high-density, high-speed, wide DDR SDRAM. Samsung also supports all densities of synchronous graphics RAM (SGRAM) in order to provide the highest flexibility and options to meet customer needs. Samsung's graphics memory die in multi-chip packaging has become the standard in notebook graphics solutions. These Samsung devices set the bar for the highest-performing graphics solutions in the world today.

As the world's largest supplier of static RAM, Samsung offers a complete line of application-driven products: slow (low-power) SRAM for mobile and other battery-operated applications; fast SRAM for the consumer market; and synchronous Single-Data-Rate and Double-Data-Rate SRAM for the cache and data communications market. Samsung's synchronous SRAM is one of the fastest devices available; its NtRAM™ (No-Turn-Around Random Access Memory) is for the networking and communications market.

Samsung has strong roots in the mass storage markets. Its NAND Flash

Samsung Semiconductor, Inc. headquarters in San Jose, California

Engineering samples of the world's first 4Gb DRAM chips debut utilizing .10-micron design.

product line services the image, voice, and data storage segments with an extensive range of products in full production. Samsung's NAND Flash components are offered in TSOP packages as well as in thin and small form factor SmartMedia™ cards (SSFDC). These components are designed for digital cameras, MP3 players, and handheld products that require removable storage. A full range of NOR Flash products is currently under development.

Samsung is also an industry leader in the Mask ROM area, supporting consumer markets with standard products and the office automation market with page mode devices. In early 1998, Samsung defined the synchronous Mask ROM, which has quickly become an industry standard. Synchronous Mask ROM provides higher bandwidth solutions for new-generation printers and personal digital assistants (PDAs).

As part of its product line, Samsung offers a broad range of microcontroller families. These MCUs are ideal for applications requiring low operating voltages and low current draw. Applications ranging from consumer products and computer peripherals to industrial and telecommunication applications have been designed using Samsung's MCUs.

Samsung's expanding MCU lines consist of a low- and high-end 4-bit family, a low- and high-end 8-bit family, and a low- and high-end 32-bit family. All are based on an advanced CMOS process technology with small feature sizes and offer very cost-effective solutions.

Samsung's multimedia product family includes solutions for video and audio applications. The company's video encoder and decoder ICs offer full-featured support for interfacing with analog video standards. High signal quality allows a diverse set of applications. Audio products integrate wavetable-based audio for unmatched MIDI-based playback.

Samsung's ASIC philosophy is to provide true "System-on-Chip" solutions with advanced memories, such as embedded DRAM, embedded Flash, embedded SRAM, and functional and analog/mixed signal IPs. This philosophy covers all the bases: from a comprehensive product portfolio to deep-sub-micron technology to macro libraries, EDA tools, and software development tools to engineering services, packaging expertise, and volume production.

Four Samsung fabrication lines are dedicated to sub-micron ASIC technology. Regional ASIC design centers provide on-staff engineers and customer-focused teams experienced in technical and risk analysis. At every step in the process, Samsung engineers help evaluate trade-offs in cost, performance, and cycle time. The company's "total solution" approach and its flexibility are helping designers move high-integration ASIC designs into the new millennium with Samsung's Intelligence-On-Silicon™.

Marketed under the WiseView™ brand, Samsung TFT-LCD displays have won worldwide recognition for their wide viewing angles, high brightness, high color depth, small form factor, and light weight. Samsung has been the market leader for laptop computer displays since 1998, and achieved that leadership position by offering top quality, advanced technologies, the highest-volume, fully automated production, and unmatched vertical integration. In the year 2000, Samsung achieved or maintained "best supplier status" with leading-edge personal computer companies such as Dell, IBM, Compaq, and Apple.

Technological innovations Samsung has achieved include the company's patented Patterned Vertical Alignment (PVA™) technology. The use of PVA enables Samsung to achieve a very high contrast wide-angle picture with television picture rates.

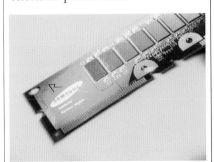

High-speed memory is a Samsung specialty as typified by the RDRAM module shown here.

As the world's largest supplier of large-size TFT-LCD displays for the industrial market, Samsung offers an extensive range of high-resolution products ranging from 12.1" all the way up to 24.0" and 30.0" TFT-LCDs. Recent technology advances have resulted in Samsung also entering the small-size TFT-LCD market with a range of small high-contrast, full-color displays. Starting at the 2.0" size, these displays specifically target the burgeoning personal digital assistant and mobile phone markets. The company's new 2.0" display can reproduce moving pictures in full color. Samsung is the first to apply low-temperature poly-silicon TFT-LCD technology to a display for mobile applications.

In addition to research, Samsung Semiconductor also invests in people and communities. The company is a major contributor to San Jose civic events and supports worthy causes that benefit the region. The division's efforts to promote employee volunteerism and to serve local needs were recently recognized with the Award for Excellence in Corporate Community Service from the Points of Light Foundation, based in Washington, D.C. Samsung's management believes that quality, service, reliability, and achievement are important values for both business and civic endeavors.

Samsung Semiconductor, Inc.
3655 North First Street
San Jose, California 95134 USA
Phone: 408.544.4000
Fax: 408.544.4980
http://www.usa.samsungsemi.com

MENTOR GRAPHICS CORPORATION

www.mentor.com

As you work away on your computer or talk on a cell phone, have you ever wondered how engineers were able to design that wondrous thing? If you have, you've wondered about the world of electronic design automation, or EDA. EDA solutions give engineers the ability to develop, test, and revise electronic designs to make certain that they function properly—and to get today's complex electronic products to market as quickly and cost-effectively as possible.

Designing ever more powerful and ever more functional electronic devices, however, is becoming more and more of a challenge. The demand is strong for products that are not only higher performing and less expensive, but also smaller and more portable. This means that engineers must adopt processes and tools that enable overall system design as well as "deep submicron" design, or design miniaturization. Their tools must also let them compress an entire electronic system onto one or more chips—what's known as "system-on-chip," or "SoC," design. And those SoCs must then be efficiently placed on printed circuit boards (PCBs) that need to perform accurately at high speeds.

Mentor Graphics® Corporation, with worldwide headquarters in Wilsonville, Oregon, and San Jose, California, is at the forefront of electronic design automation. Mentor was a pioneer in the EDA industry when the company was founded in 1981. At the start of the new millennium, it is an industry leader. With President and CEO Walden C. Rhines at the helm, Mentor Graphics offers a wide variety of innovative and effective solutions that help engineers overcome tough design obstacles and produce electronic devices that meet consumer needs. The company's expertise includes SoC design; PCB design; field programmable gate array (FPGA) design, which uses a programmable kind of integrated circuit; and physical verification and analysis, which checks whether a design will actually function when placed on silicon.

SoC design is a new way of looking at the function, and therefore the design, of a chip. Because of size and function demands, a complete silicon system—microprocessor, memory, logic, and embedded software—must now be contained on one or more chips. And these chips must co-exist and communicate with a printed circuit board. Engineers, therefore, need a design environment that lets them take components from multiple sources, integrate them, and then test them so that they can catch any design flaws while they're still easy to fix. Mentor Graphics is the leading company providing a complete solution for this type of design flow.

Printed circuit boards, on which chips are placed, also present design problems. These range from the challenging physical effects of high-speed boards to the difficulties of data and process management when design teams in diverse geographies work concurrently on a project. Mentor Graphics provides design solutions to enable fast and right-first-time design of the boards that are the backbones of a host of electronic products.

More and more of these products are being produced with FPGAs, which are becoming larger and more complex. Mentor provides a suite of design tools that enable engineers to capture a design concept in graphical form, simulate its operation, and convert text description into working circuit parts.

Physical verification is the final step in design, before manufacturing begins. Each electronic system design must not only perform reliably, but must also meet manufacturing requirements. Shrinking physical size and growing density are formidable obstacles to meeting these requirements, and mistakes or delays at this stage of the process are not only costly but can cause a company to lose its edge in the marketplace. Mentor Graphics provides physical verification software that is recognized as unquestionably the best in the industry. It has been adopted unanimously by all the major chip-producing foundries.

Mentor Graphics improves and simplifies the entire design process to fuel electronics innovation and help customers capitalize on new markets as Internet, computer, communications, and consumer applications converge. New technologies are profoundly changing the way engineers are designing the next generation of electronics, and Mentor Graphics design automation software is enabling its customers to turn today's engineering ideas into tomorrow's hot products.

Mentor Graphics®

LINEAR TECHNOLOGY

www.linear.com

If you've ever surfed the Net, used a desktop or portable computer, talked on a cell phone, or had a dashboard device tell you how to get where you're going—or just turned up the radio volume or dimmed the lights in the living room—you've reaped the kind of benefits made possible by the high-performance products of Linear Technology. Based in Milpitas, California, Linear, led by CEO Robert Swanson, designs and manufactures a diverse line of analog, or linear, integrated circuits that play crucial roles in digital devices such as cellular phones and laptop computers.

While digital circuits generally process on-off electrical signals involved in computational functions, analog circuits monitor, condition (make more able to transmit data), amplify, or transform continuous analog signals associated with the real-world physical properties of temperature, pressure, weight, position, light, sound, and speed. In other words, analog circuits act as a bridge between the electronic world and the real world—they allow people to put digital devices to practical use.

Many of those uses are in the field of computer networking, including the World Wide Web. The ease with which we find or send a particular piece of information or order a book, toy, or groceries online is made possible through a series of complex routers, switches, and systems that filter, convert, and manage the data we need. In these

Robert Swanson, founder and CEO of Linear Technology

networks, high-performance analog integrated circuits perform monitoring and control functions, route processing, cable management, and power switching. They're part of the electronic "nuts and bolts" that make networking work.

Linear's high-power, high-speed integrated circuits are also found in the fast-growing world of wireless communication. "Information appliances" such as cellular telephones, laptop computers, and Global Positioning Systems offer significant benefits, but they impose enormous challenges to power management and signal processing. Linear's integrated circuits meet this

demand with a wide range of new devices. These products extend battery life, reduce charging time, increase processing power, and make possible smaller-sized devices that provide greater user flexibility and satisfaction. For example, thanks to analog circuitry, cell phones function up to eight hours instead of running out of battery power in two, and notebook computers operate for the length of a cross-country flight.

Travelers also enjoy the benefits of other electronic products enhanced by analog technology. Analog components capture directional beacons, lock onto signals, extract data, and display data that provide comfort and safety in automobiles, planes, boats, and trains. City buses tracked by analog-aided Global Positioning Systems more routinely arrive at their posted times.

Systems that monitor the wear and tear of engines provide better preventive maintenance models and equipment reliability. New technology is also advancing collision avoidance and other in-car pluses such as maps on demand and e-mail delivery.

Linear Technology is also working closely with companies in the medical electronics fields. For example, their operational amplifiers, monolithic filters, and digital-to-analog filters are key to analytic devices such as instruments used for DNA testing. Their products also make possible the economical miniaturization of sensors, motors, radios, and monitors—devices that gather important diagnostic information that is crucial to our health and well-being.

CYPRESS SEMICONDUCTOR

www.cypress.com

For more than a decade following its 1982 beginnings, Cypress Semiconductor was at the forefront of the huge expansion in the semiconductor market. The groundbreaking CMOS (complementary metal oxide semiconductor) processing technology the company introduced produced integrated circuits that were faster, cheaper to make, and consumed less power. Its flagship SRAM (static random access memory) product was in great demand for the electronic devices that were becoming more and more a part of everyday life.

Cypress's Fab I is the company's first fab, located on the headquarters campus. It is the focus of Cypress's R&D efforts, manufacturing advanced technology products.

By the mid-'90s, however, dozens of companies had entered the SRAM market, stiffening competition and driving prices down. T. J. Rodgers, Cypress's founder and current president and CEO, knew it was time to make a change, and decided to point his company in a new direction. Cypress began to aim at high-volume, fast-growing markets, particularly in the communications sector. Today the international company, whose corporate headquarters are in San Jose, California, is "Driving the Communications Revolution.™" Cypress has more than a billion dollars in revenues, the vast majority derived from devices that are used widely in wireless handsets (cell phones), wireless base stations, and wide-area and storage-area networks (systems that move and store Internet data). The company's products are in demand by such industry giants as Alcatel, Cisco, Ericsson, Lucent, Motorola, Nortel Networks, and 3Com.

Cypress produces state-of-the art memory devices focused largely in two areas: wireless and networking. Its low-power MoBL™ (More Battery Life™) SRAMs are used in mobile applications such as cellular phones that need extended battery power and more talk time. On the networking side, Cypress's super-fast QDR™ (Quad Data Rate™) memories support next-generation switches and routers that move terabytes of data across the Internet in the blink of an eye. Its QuadPort™ RAM memory product has four independent ports that can simultaneously provide access to data, alleviating network bottlenecks.

A full range of non-memory products are also part of Cypress's networking portfolio, including an OC-48 "physical layer" that transmits and receives data at 2.5 gigabits per second over a fiber network. The company's PSI™ (Programmable Serial Interface) chip family flexibly moves data at high speeds in serial backplane (specially designed interconnecting device) applications.

Through a spate of recent acquisitions, Cypress has moved into additional fast-growing areas. Its purchases of Alation and RadioCom have provided the company with the critical technologies needed for Bluetooth, a standard communications link for wireless terminals, PCs, and other devices. Its acquisition of Silicon Light Machines has positioned Cypress at the leading edge of opto-electronics, an exciting emerging technology that converts digital data into light and back again in high-speed switches and other applications. Many believe that opto-electronics will be the next great frontier for the semiconductor industry.

Because there is great demand on system designers to bring new products to market quickly, Cypress also produces complex programmable logic devices (CPLDs). These products can be custom programmed by engineers as systems are developed and logic changes need to be made. Cypress's newest CPLD family, the Delta39K™, offers CPLDs that are several times larger than competitors', increasing system performance in a range of communication applications.

Because digital system performance is continuing to grow, system timing is becoming ever more critical to the success of new electronic product design. Cypress offers a broad array of timing solutions for the wireless, networking, consumer, and computation markets. The company is number one in the timing technology business, and is also number one in USB sales. Cypress produces a complete family of USB chips for use in PC peripherals, such as mice, keyboards, digital cameras, and disk drives.

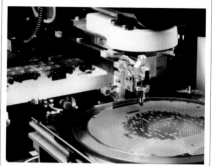

Wafer manufacturing at Cypress Semiconductor

Cypress's management believes that much of the company's success is due to its ability to manufacture its products quickly and cost effectively, using the latest process technology. The company has wafer manufacturing plants in California, Minnesota, and Texas, and an advanced test-and-assembly facility in the Philippines. But manufacturing products that are key elements in devices developed by the leading datacom and telecom companies is the way its expertise reaches and benefits the public. At the start of the new century, Cypress is paving the "information superhighway" with silicon, and is on its way to fulfilling its two goals: to become the preferred silicon supplier for Internet switching systems, and to have every Internet data stream pass through at least one of its integrated circuits.

ASYST TECHNOLOGIES

www.asyst.com

No matter where we live or what we do, semiconductor-based electronics are becoming a bigger and bigger part of our lives. And with amazing speed these invaluable machines are growing increasingly sophisticated and powerful. But to create these wondrous new products, more streamlined and more effective manufacturing processes and environments are needed to build the complex integrated circuits (ICs) that run them.

For many years, ICs have been processed and manufactured in "cleanrooms"—large rooms in which damage-causing contaminants such as dust are kept down as much as possible. To increase cleanroom effectiveness, Asyst Technologies, Inc., of Fremont, California, developed a revolutionary technology. In effect they miniaturized the cleanroom with automation, making it necessary to control contaminants just in the immediate areas in which semiconductor wafers are processed. Asyst also developed additional isolation, automation, and material management "minienvironment" technologies.

Why are Asyst's products and technologies so important? Because they help IC and other high-tech manufacturers produce high chip yields, a key to profitability. With each new generation of semiconductor wafers, human, environmental, and technical hazards have increased exponentially during production. At the same time, performance enhancements have

Dr. Mihir Parikh, chairman and chief executive officer of Asyst

increased wafer value. Today, for example, a single production wafer that contains microprocessors is worth more than $100,000—10 times what it was worth 10 years ago. When you multiply that figure by 250,000 to 500,000—the number of wafers the average fabrication plant starts to build in a year—it's easy to see the importance of assuring defect-free wafer production.

Asyst's minienvironment solutions also benefit chip production workers. For example, large cleanrooms require operators to move in-process wafers through many pieces of equipment and through a large number of processing steps. One type of integrated circuit fabrication, called Very Large Scale Integration, requires operators to move batches of silicon wafers in cassettes through more than 100 pieces of processing equipment and over 500 processing steps. But the Asyst-SMIF System™ is completely automated. SMIF, which stands for Standard Mechanical InterFace, uses specially constructed sealed containers, called

SMIF-Pods™, to enclose wafer cassettes. Ultraclean air is delivered directly into each breadbox-size enclosure, keeping out the contaminants that can damage wafer surfaces and make the devices on wafers inoperable. Robotic arms remove the cassettes from their enclosures and load them into and out of processing equipment without exposing them to outside air.

In addition to its minienvironment system, Asyst also produces a system for tracking and controlling wafers as they move around the fabrication area. In conventional cleanrooms, batches of wafers are usually tracked by attaching barcode tags to the wafer carriers. Instead of using paper, Asyst's SMART-Traveler System™ tracks semiconductor wafers with an intelligent electronic-memory device and automated identification tags. These tools reduce manufacturing mistakes as well as improve overall fabrication efficiency.

Dr. Mihir Parikh, chairman and chief executive officer of Asyst, believes his company's technologies are of great benefit to semiconductor manufacturers and, therefore, to consumers. State-of-the-art processing and factory automation, he states, are critical in helping chip makers meet both their technology and their manufacturing goals. Not only have manufacturers who use Asyst's technologies saved millions in production and construction costs, but their product quality has also increased. Equally important in today's tight and competitive labor market, cleanrooms have become much more "user friendly." Workers no longer have

to wear the awkward, contamination-reducing "bunny suits" of the past. Now, because only the small enclosures must be kept superclean, operators can dress in more comfortable, less confining clothes and headgear.

For the past 15 years, Asyst's mission has been to assure the quality of semiconductor wafers as they move through the manufacturing cycle. That goal will remain at the forefront as more advanced circuits require wafer size changes—from 200 mm (8 in.) to 300 mm (12 in.)—doubling the number of devices at risk on any one wafer at any one processing step. With Asyst's isolation technology, it's more likely that the innovative electronic products of the future that will require advanced circuits will be reliable and affordable. Asyst's technologies are currently being considered for use in producing disk drives and flat-panel displays, and in the pharmaceutical and biomedical fields.

VersaPort™ 2200

VISHAY INTERTECHNOLOGY, INC.

www.vishay.com
www.siliconix.com

When he emigrated to the United States from his native Poland, chairman and CEO of Vishay Intertechnology Dr. Felix Zandman put his education in higher mathematics and physics right to work. He developed a special industrial coating that, when applied to a structure and viewed through a device that polarized light, measured the stress on that structure. His research in this area led him to develop the Bulk Metal® foil resistor, an ultra-precise, ultra-stable electronic component that remains the highest-performing resistor today. And that innovation led him to found his own company in 1962 to further develop and manufacture Bulk Metal resistors. Dr. Zandman named his new company Vishay, the name of the Lithuanian village where his grandmother had lived, in honor of family members who died in the Holocaust.

Today, Vishay Intertechnology, with headquarters in Malvern, Pennsylvania, is the largest U.S. and European manufacturer of passive electronic components and a major producer of discrete semiconductors and selected integrated circuits (ICs). Passive components include resistors, which control the flow of electrical current; capacitors, which stop the flow of DC current but allow AC current to flow; and inductors, which control AC current and voltage. They're all called passive because they do not amplify DC current or voltage.

Because of its purchase in the late 1990s of several companies, including 80.4% of Santa Clara, California–based Siliconix, Vishay is a major producer of semiconductors. These active electronic components, or power semiconductor products, from Siliconix are used to switch and convert power in a wide range of systems, from portable information appliances to the communications infrastructure that enables the Internet. The company's power MOSFETs—tiny solid-state switches, or metal oxide semiconductor field-effect transistors—and power integrated circuits are widely used in cell phones and notebook computers to manage battery power efficiently, directing power where it's needed or converting it to the right

PowerPAK™ power MOSFET packaging technology from Siliconix Incorporated (NASDAQ: SILI), an 80.4%-owned subsidiary of Vishay Intertechnology, Inc. (NYSE: VSH), advances thermal conductivity by an order of magnitude while providing dramatic space savings for high power density applications.

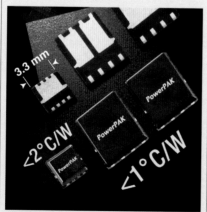

voltage level for digital components. Power MOSFETs are also used to drive motors, for example, in anti-skid braking and electric steering systems in automobiles. Siliconix also manufactures a large family of analog signal processing components that are used in instrumentation, communication, entertainment, and many other applications. Other semiconductor products from Vishay include Vishay Telefunken diodes, opto-electronics, radio-frequency transistors, and infrared data communications transceivers.

Like Vishay, Siliconix has a long and illustrious corporate history. Also founded in 1962, Siliconix was the vision of Frances and Bill Hugle, research scientists whose first products were junction field-effect transistors (JFETs). Such transistors are low-noise devices that switch and sense analog signals. In 1963, the company began shipping its first integrated circuits, and now has a worldwide reputation for innovation in power ICs and power MOSFETs. Its newest LITTLE FOOT® power MOSFETs pack more than two million transistor cells in a 1.8 mm by 1.1 mm piece of silicon, reducing the board space needed in portable electronics while ensuring efficient, effective power management.

With the wide-ranging products and services Siliconix brought to the merger, Vishay Intertechnology is now one of the few companies that can design and manufacture a complete package of active and passive components for almost any electronic application. For example, they can supply the passive components,

Dr. Felix Zandman, chairman and CEO of Vishay Intertechnology, Inc.

semiconductors, and infrared transceiver—a device that is beginning to replace the cable connections between laptops, cell phones, and digital cameras—that are found in a typical cell phone.

In addition to cell phones, Vishay's products go into numerous devices that are part of the surging telecommunications industry. These include hand-held global positioning systems and child locators, as well as caller ID and voice-activated dialing equipment. Its resistors, capacitors, diodes, and transceivers are advancing miniaturization, higher efficiency, extended run times, and wireless connections. Its power integrated circuits are saving space, promoting better use of battery power, enabling new features, and making devices more user friendly. And its power MOSFETs consume considerably less power as they perform their functions. This means that battery-powered devices have extended lives and can include more useful features.

Printers and scanners are another

New low-threshold small-signal MOSFETs from Vishay are packaged in the tiny SC-70 and feature a maximum gate-threshold voltage of just 1.5 V.

area in which Vishay products are improving performance. Working with Hewlett-Packard, Vishay developed seven optical sensors that use little power and take up minimal space. Three of the sensors control printer paper insertion and sorting while another regulates the paper supply. Additional sensors handle the material to be printed and detect how color is being positioned to provide the best possible print quality. A media sensor, which is used in scanners, helps determine what kind of image is being scanned and then imaged on the monitor for further processing.

As in the cell phone, a large number of Vishay components can be found in the typical computer. As processing speeds increase and features become more advanced, there is an ever-greater need for passive components and semiconductors. For example, the first Pentium® processor required 252 passive components. The much more powerful Pentium III requires 440 passive components. In the portable computer world, Vishay products are also supporting increased performance. Their components are meeting the latest miniaturization challenges, reducing battery-recharging time, and allowing battery power to be used more efficiently.

In automobiles, too, the demand for electronic components continues to increase. More and more of a car's subsystems are going from mechanical to electronic operation, including engine control, climate control, and air bag deployment. Plus, manufacturers are constantly adding and improving capabilities. Upgrades in automatic braking systems, remote security devices, and automatic transmission selection—known as "drive-by-wire" technology—are continually being designed. And drivers and passengers continue to ask for more convenience and more comfort on the road.

What all of this means is that designers are in need of more and more rugged, quality components that can withstand the high temperatures under which cars and trucks must operate. It also means that they need reliable components, because automotive parts that fail can result in catastrophe. Vishay provides both traditional and surface-mount components—surface-mount components deliver greater functionality in less space—that meet industry standards. These products include multilayer ceramic capacitors, air bag fuse resistors, infrared remote controls, and analog switches. Its sensor products can be found in the advanced rain sensors that adapt windshield wiper speed to varying rain intensity, and in the electronic fuel-level sensors that tell you when you need to get gas. Additional products can be found in other vehicle systems, including lighting, steering, and suspension.

The worldwide market for military and aerospace equipment is another area in which Vishay is a major supplier. Its military and aerospace components are designed to withstand the extreme heat and cold of outer space, as well as intense vibrations and other environmental stresses. Just like automotive components, these components go through significant testing and failure analysis to meet the great need for quality and reliability. The company also designs custom components for use in such applications as missile systems and ground-based communications systems. Vishay products also will be part of the several hundred space platforms that are expected to be launched by 2005. These platforms will provide commercial telephone, satellite TV, and data services back on Earth.

In the medical sector, the need for computerized control of instruments and equipment is increasing, and here again Vishay is supplying critical components. The company is working with product designers to advance subsystems such as power management and to make tools smaller, lighter, and less costly. It is also working toward increasing performance in test and measurement equipment and the mobile equipment that lets health care providers monitor patients over wireless data networks. Its components can be found in pacemakers and other implantable devices where long-term performance and reliability are a must.

Though Vishay already produces the passive and active components that electronics manufacturers need for today's electronic systems, the company is not resting on its laurels. Its constant investment in research and development results in a steady stream of new products—150 in 1999 alone, including 67 new MOSFETs. These products are making possible more advanced cell phones, lighter and higher-performing laptops, more reliable automotive systems, miniaturized surgical instruments, and much more. Its Quality program is also paving the way for more reliable electronic devices by rigorously monitoring all manufacturing processes. The company's goal is to exceed the quality expectations of its customers and to meet the continuing global demand for higher-performing, more reliable electronic solutions.

Si9731DQ microprocessor-controlled battery charger IC in TSSOP-16, from Siliconix Incorporated (NASDAQ: SILI), an 80.4%-owned subsidiary of Vishay Intertechnology, Inc. (NYSE: VSH), is a space-saving solution for lithium ion or nickel battery designs, eliminating the need for several external components in cell phones, PDAs, and other hand-held appliances.

INFINEON TECHNOLOGIES

www.infineon.com

Never stop thinking—about improvement and change, about the future, about shaping new industries. Infineon Technologies' slogan aptly summarizes the company's commitment to meeting and exceeding the needs of its customers and to producing higher-performing, state-of-the-art chips for a variety of semiconductor markets. Always thinking about growth and quality has enabled the company, led by president and CEO Dr. Ulrich Schumacher, to become one of the leading chip manufacturers in the world.

This 1 Gigabyte module provides unprecedented memory capacity for computer workstations and servers.

Infineon Technologies designs, produces, and markets semiconductors for wired and wireless communication, automotive uses, and computer products. The company was founded on April 1, 1999, when the semiconductor business of parent company Siemens AG was placed under Infineon's roof. The establishment of the new company enabled Infineon to be more flexible in the highly technical and highly competitive semiconductor industry, and to become one of the top 10 ranked companies within it.

Infineon's 29,000 employees are located in offices and research facilities across the globe but focus their work on five different customer-oriented business units. The Wireless Products unit produces semiconductors and complete system solutions for a range of wireless applications, including cellular and cordless telephone systems and devices used in connection with global positioning systems. Products include standardized baseband ICs (logic and analog) and standardized and customized radio frequency ICs. In fact, the company's product range is so wide in this area that Infineon can supply just about every essential component needed to build a digital mobile phone, from battery to microphone to antenna. And, as cell phones become lighter and more compact, Infineon is committed to providing its customers with even more miniaturized circuitry. The company is also working toward a transition to multimedia-capable cell phone systems.

With multimedia documents becoming more and more important, the amount of data being transmitted requires ever-increasing bandwidth. This in turn requires higher-performing chips, in particular in the area of high-speed communication via fiberglass and DSL networks. The Communications unit provides system-on-chip solutions for a wide variety of multimedia applications, including integrated circuits for digital speech, data, and video transmission; signal processors and controllers for data services; set-top boxes; and integrated circuits for fiber optics and high-speed networking. Semiconductors and systems are produced for wired communication based on television (cable), PC (LAN), or wired telephony technologies. Products also

Low-power, high-density Mobile RAM dramatically improves battery life in portable devices.

include optic components and infrared components.

A third business unit, Automotive and Industrial, produces power semiconductors, opto components, microcontrollers, sensors, and discrete semiconductors for a full range of automotive and machine applications. The chips this unit supplies enable advanced automotive solutions for power train management; safety systems, including intelligent air bags; convenience features, such as power windows; driver information systems, such as navigation systems and satellite positioning; and in-car entertainment systems. Industrial chip applications include sensors, machine construction, control technology, and household appliances.

The Security and Chip Card ICs division has made Infineon the leading global supplier of chip card integrated circuits. The intelligent chip card, known as the Smart Card, is one of the most promising solutions for guaranteeing the security of electronically transmitted information, since it is capable of identifying a user and protecting electronic documents from unauthorized access. Currently, the

Security and Chip Card ICs division develops and manufactures security controllers, security monitors, and other semiconductors for use in telephone and credit cards, health and ID cards, pay TV, and traffic control applications. One of Infineon's newest technologies, the Fingertip™ sensor, is enabling a new range of identification solutions.

Infineon's Memory Products unit develops and produces DRAM (dynamic random access memory) storage chips of up to 1 gigabit. These chips are used to store information in a full range of electronic equipment, including desktop and laptop computers, servers, printers, video recorders, car radios, and answering machines. The company's innovative technology has produced a new technique for manufacturing DRAMs on 300-millimeter (12-inch) wafers, and the first available working DRAMs of this size were produced at the company's Dresden, Germany, facility. Infineon has wide experience with memory products and will be focusing on function- and application-specific integrated circuits for products in the growing intellectual

"Smart Cards" use Infineon chips to secure electronic identities, enabling financial services and new e-commerce capabilities.

Digital Subscriber Line (DSL) chipset technology turns copper phone wires into broadband data and voice pipelines.

property arena.

Though the company is headquartered in Munich, Germany, one of its premier research and development operations is located in San Jose, California. R&D efforts at this site, and at Infineon's 15 additional research facilities, which together are known as the Competence Network, concentrate on developing better and more comprehensive solutions for increasingly complex applications. This means working to meet the IC needs of customers whose electronic devices are becoming smaller, lighter, and more mobile, and meeting the needs of users who demand more power and performance. In order to reach these goals, Infineon has entered into numerous partnerships and production relationships with such industry leaders as IBM, Motorola, Nokia, and Sun Microsystems.

Continuing its concentration on providing state-of-the-art communication ICs, Infineon announced the availability of the first chipset, or collection of chips that work together to perform a function, integrating voice and digital phone standard ADSL (asymmetric digital subscriber line) services on a single line card. This breakthrough eliminates the need for splitters on a network, and enables mass provisioning of the speedy ADSL service to a network. The new product offers service providers a quick and easy way to upgrade access network systems and provide converged voice and data services.

Another new Infineon product is known as TSLP, or Thin Small Leadless Package. This recent innovation is a plastic, lead-less package for discrete semiconductor devices that is only 1 x

.6 x .4 mm. in size. The ultra-miniature housing is approximately 20% the size of a standard package and can hold a wide variety of diodes and transistors. The greatly reduced package footprint is ideal for applications that require extreme component miniaturization, such as wireless systems, personal digital assistants, digital cameras, and portable digital audio/video players. Diodes and transistors that use TSLP also show an improved frequency response.

In addition to making research and development a priority, Infineon also looks ahead to new markets and new industries. In 1998, Infineon Ventures was established to invest in and shape new microelectronics opportunities, leveraging its technologies, applications, and market experience to companies worldwide. With offices in Munich and San Jose, Infineon Ventures focuses on developments in networking ICs, optical networking, network security, wireless Internet solutions, and multimedia solutions.

As microelectronics proliferate, the need for high-performing, miniaturized components is greater than ever before. These building blocks—for our computers, cell phones, digital TVs, jet planes, pacemakers, automobiles, and ATM machines—must be reliable, affordable, and available for the many tasks that require them. They must also change and improve as new developments in electronics occur. Today the staff of Infineon Technologies is working to meet these needs, and continually thinking about new ways to optimize chip performance tomorrow.

ATMEL CORPORATION

www.atmel.com

E-commerce. Laptop computers. Digital cameras. Mobile phones. Though you may not know they're there, Atmel's chips and system solutions are at the heart of today's latest electronic products and services. The company's unusually broad range of chips, devices, and technologies enables an unusually broad range of customers to develop high-performing, highly beneficial products.

Though its name came from the words advanced technology for memory and logic, Atmel has been repositioning itself to widen its focus from stand-alone memory. Today the company is a leading designer and manufacturer of a broad range of advanced semiconductors, including logic, non-volatile memory (the kind of memory that gives electronic devices the ability to retain information even after power is turned off), mixed signal circuits, and radio frequency integrated circuits. Atmel, which is headquartered in San Jose, California, is also a leading provider of system-level integrated solutions. That means the company develops circuits that integrate low-power logic operations with non-volatile memory. Atmel is one of only a few companies capable of integrating non-volatile memory with logic and analog functions on a single chip. It is also able to "mix and match" any combination of logic, non-volatile memory, mixed signal, and radio frequency functions.

Using its cutting-edge semiconductor technology, Atmel has enabled its customers to combine a variety of digital and analog functions on a single piece of silicon. This technology, known as "system on chip" (SoC), reduces power-consumption package size and cost, both of which are essential for products designed for the mobile market.

Atmel has used its own SoC technology to produce a highly integrated biometric fingerprint sensor. This product, known as FingerChip™, is the smallest solid-state silicon fingerprint sensor in the world. Identification of the user is authenticated by swiping a finger over the device, giving immediate, secure access to bank accounts without the need for a PIN; opening car doors without a key; and making a purchase over the Internet using a cellular telephone. SoC technology has become essential in the development of large networking, communication, and computer systems.

Atmel also provides secure and private access to important data through its "Smart Card" integrated circuits. These ICs combine dense non-volatile memory with a flexible microcontroller and a powerful encryption engine to give users entry to their health records, Social Security records, and Internet shopping. But while its Smart Card and FingerChip circuits give people easy access to information, a cryptographic processor Atmel has developed protects against hacker access to secret information. As part of a turnkey hardware solution developed with IBM, this innovation provides a high level of security for computer users who exchange e-mail or do business over the Internet.

As in the Smart Card, the microcontroller is the "brains" behind the control function in virtually all electronic and electrically powered systems. Atmel manufactures the industry's widest range of in-system programmable Flash memory microcontrollers; on-board Flash allows the device to be reprogrammed without the need to remove it from the system. Atmel's newest Flash-based microcontroller provides up to 10 times the performance of the previous model and requires one-tenth the power.

Atmel is also one of the first manufacturers to introduce integrated circuits that meet the Bluetooth specification. Bluetooth is a worldwide open standard that supports short-range wireless communication between such products as computers, mobile phones, personal digital applications, and headsets. Atmel's ICs enable system designers to effect wireless transfer of voice and data, which enables users to make instant, cable-free connections among electronic devices.

George Perlegos, founder, president, and chief executive officer of Atmel, feels that the company's new direction has produced many new products that are advancing the interconnected world. From wireless telecommunication to consumer electronics to e-commerce transactions, Atmel's "building blocks" have helped customers produce state-of-the-art devices that offer greater performance at a lower price, smaller size, longer battery life, and more memory. In addition, by combining memory and a microcontroller on a single chip, the company has enabled wireless and portable products to be designed more quickly and more cost effectively. Atmel produces and ships more than four million ICs a day—more than a billion a year. Though you may not see them, they are a big part of our electronic world.

The 32 Mb AT49LD3200 and AT49LD3200B are the first two members of the SFlash™ family that operate at frequencies up to 100 MHz and are organized x16/x32. SFlash allows system designers utilizing SDRAM to incorporate a high-speed, execute-in-place (XIP) Flash memory onto the same bus. This potentially eliminates the asynchronous memory bus and the associated interface pins and control logic. SFlash is a very attractive solution for performance-oriented applications such as printers, networking products, set-top boxes, digital televisions, and car navigation systems.

FLEXTRONICS INTERNATIONAL LTD.

www.flextronics.com

When the company he worked for went out of business, Joe McKenzie might have been discouraged. But the loss of his job turned out to be a positive career step. It led him to found Flextronics, which is now a $12 billion global electronics force.

When McKenzie started Flextronics, the service he provided was called "board stuffing." This meant the company handled the overflow manufacturing needs of companies that needed more circuit boards than they could produce themselves; Flextronics employees mounted and hand-soldered the parts into place. The business became successful, and was bought in 1980 by Bob Todd, Joe Sullivan, and Jack Watts. Todd took over as CEO, and started the company on its way to becoming the powerhouse electronics manufacturing services (EMS) provider it is today.

Now headquartered in Singapore, with regional headquarters in San Jose,

CEO Michael Marks on the production floor

California, Western Europe, and Asia, Flextronics International is currently headed by chairman and CEO Michael E. Marks. Under his leadership, the company provides flexible and fast design, engineering, and manufacturing services to original equipment manufacturers (OEMs) in the fast-growing communications, networking, computer, medical, and consumer markets. Flextronics gives its customers what it calls a total global manufacturing solution.

In today's fast-paced world, product manufacturers are being asked to deliver more quickly and to respond immediately to changes in consumer demand. Flextronics is providing these manufacturers with the resources they need to maintain their competitive edge and to react with speed and accuracy. By offering a full-service, one-stop solution, Flextronics is enabling its OEM customers to lower the cost of manufacturing and transporting their products. It is also increasing customers' ability to reach consumers worldwide.

At the core of Flextronics' ability to provide its customers with complete, high-volume, electronic manufacturing services are the company's revolutionary Industrial Parks. These complexes are unique in that they house both the suppliers and the product assembly facilities on the same campus. Raw materials, components, and sub-assemblies are put together into finished products and then distributed worldwide. Using the Industrial Park model, customers reduce their travel and transport costs, share overhead costs, have

better communication with partners, see faster turnaround times, and have access to a larger pool of manufacturing expertise. Additionally, suppliers are free to work with other companies, allowing a win-win situation for both parties. Flextronics Industrial Parks are located in Asia, Europe, and North and South America.

Another key element in Flextronics' total manufacturing solution is the company's Product Introduction Centers (PICs). As technology becomes increasingly complex and competition among manufacturers intensifies, OEMs need to know their products will perform at their best the first time out. The engineers at the Product Introduction Centers design new products, develop prototypes, then test and launch the devices. These services shorten development time and give customers a leading edge. The PICs offer engineering, layout, simulation, and prototype services, and engineers recommend the right technology to suit the manufacture of each product.

While Flextronics has provided wide-reaching manufacturing services through its Plastics, Semiconductors, Design, Networking, and PCB (printed circuit board) Fabrication business units, it recently added two business units that will increase the company's capabilities. The Photonics business unit offers design, industrialization, supply chain management, and manufacturing services to optical component and optical networking organizations. The Enclosures business unit provides design, manufacturing, integration,

Overview of production floor

and deployment services, supplying custom electronic enclosures to the communications infrastructure, computer, and networking industries. The division provides entire systems, including the enclosure, the power system, cable assemblies, and drives.

With each of Flextronics' additions and improvements, the company is moving steadily toward its goal of providing flexible, fast, "end to end" solutions for its customers. This involves having the ability to take customer orders, manufacture entire products in any part of the world, and then get those products into the hands of those who will use them. In pursuit of that goal, Flextronics is investing heavily in creating tools that manage information. For example, a system currently in use enables the company to take orders from a customer's Web site, build the products, and ship them directly to the customer. Flextronics also recently announced that it had signed the largest supply agreement in the history of the electronics industry—for $30 billion—to provide assembly, design, and infrastructure services for a major technology company across its entire product line and on every continent.

Silicon Valley Entrepreneurs: Creating a New Business Paradigm

For many years, the only way to establish a new business was to first completely learn the old—from the ground up. You would apprentice yourself to a company, the older the better; move up the ranks, from position to position; follow the boss's style and lead; and then finally, finally, have the chance for leadership yourself. This was the accepted road to ride on, and it was long and twisting and often monotonous. But it was the norm.

Then, not that long ago, a band of new riders took a look down that road and decided they didn't want to travel on it. Maybe it was the times they lived in. Maybe it was because they just didn't want to do what everyone had done before. Or maybe it was because they had ideas for new ways of doing things that they wanted people to be able to get their hands on right away. They didn't think they needed to wait. They took a fork in the road and headed for a new territory where things happened fast and where life was much more exciting—risky and exciting. They charged into Silicon Valley without much money but with determination and creativity to spare.

Failure is a prerequisite to success. At Stanford, I invented things that I was trying to use as the basis for a company, and I invented a technology, a really strange technology, which etched silicon along crystal facets and actually formed transistors in little grooved notches that were 1/100th the size of a human hair. The technology was promising. The first job I took, at American Microsystems, I worked on that technology for five years and 17 days, and I lost $20 million bucks for them and it crashed big time. So my first job was a colossal failure where we lost a lot of money.

T. J. Rodgers, Founder of Cypress Semiconductor

What is unique about Silicon Valley is the permission to fail, as long as you don't do it in too boring a way. I spent a lot of time on the East Coast, and the New York culture is very, very different. In most cases there you carry your failures with you. In Silicon Valley, it's all tied to the last thing you did or the thing you're currently on. There is no history, and I think there's a real advantage in a culture that doesn't have a history and isn't tied to history.

Steve Meyer, Founder of Atari

And Varian was established. And Hewlett-Packard, and Fairchild, and all the other innovative, groundbreaking companies founded on an idea, a dream, and a shoestring. The entrepreneurs who flocked to Silicon Valley changed the way in which careers were made. And the area welcomed them and gave them room to learn and grow.

Not every new company and new

When you grow up you tend to get told that the world is the way it is and your life is just to live your life inside the world, try not to bash in the walls too much, try to have a nice family life, have fun, save a little money, but that's a very limited life. Life can be much broader once you discover one simple fact, and that is that everything around you that you call life was made up by people who were no smarter than you, and that you can change things, you can influence things, you can build your own things that other people can use. You [need to] understand that you can poke life, you can push and something will pop out the other side, you can change life, you can mold it. That's a very important thing, to shake off this erroneous notion that life is there and you're just going to live it, when you should embrace it, change it, improve it, make your mark upon it. Once you learn that, you'll want to change life and make it better, because it's kind of messed up in a lot of ways. Once you learn that, you'll never be the same again.

Steve Jobs, Founder of Apple

---

entrepreneur became a success story. For all the remarkable successes we can name there were many, many failures. In earlier times, failure was simply not acceptable. Only if you were able to take orders and continue moving ahead under a superior's plan were you considered to be "making it." But from the start of the Silicon Valley explosion, most of the failures that took place there weren't career ending, or even viewed as failures in the traditional sense. With the new way of doing business came a new way of looking at success and failure, and realizing that failure can be a part of success. In fact, it can be a prerequisite for success. From failure we can learn, and with new information and understanding we can succeed.

Not everybody has relationships. I don't see that as something that interferes with being able to do business here. Absolutely not. No. That's one of the things that I like about this area. It is a level playing field from that perspective. You have to use your imagination. You have to get creative. I think that's one of the things that made this particular valley strong, being able to use creativity and not always repeat the same things over and over. People use their minds. They develop.

Ned Barnholt, CEO of Agilent

So the time-honored paradigm of apprenticeship went the way of the typewriter and the rotary-dial telephone. And gray hair and years at the top were no longer absolute requirements for running a successful business enterprise. Silicon Valley entrepreneurs not only blazed new paths in technology, they established new standards and procedures for running a business that would bring that technology to the public. Out with the need for a long track record and personnel file that showed carefully calculated upward movement. And in with the new way of building a career in which you take your shot, team with others to share your expertise, and learn from both your successes and your failures.

Which entrepreneur would you bet on?

1. A great salesperson with no financial or management skills

2. A great financial officer with no marketing experience

3. An inventor with no "people skills"

4. A jack-of-all-trades who learned his lessons while founding a business that ultimately failed because of external factors (recession, loss of location, etc.)

We all used to talk about our forward visibility—we planned out three years or four years, and the classic was a five-year business plan. Today, anyone in this industry who says they can see more than 18 months ahead is kidding you. I mean, the rate of speed is just too fast. It's like coming down a double black-diamond run. You're trying to look as far ahead as you can, but the speed at which you're moving and the topography are changing all the time. You just can't see all the twists and turns.

David Peterschmidt, CEO of Inktomi

The next 10, 20 years will be an absolutely brilliant time for major, major discoveries in technology fields. So I am extremely happy with the opportunity that I've been given. I've been involved in seven different enterprises since 1961, and although not all of them have been successful, the contributions that have been made through the majority of them that have succeeded have been a tremendous reward in my life. Although at this particular time I'm in a mature stage of my life, I feel like I'm just at the very beginning. I guess that this environment makes you feel of a young mind—you go beyond the physical age processes that might limit you. I don't feel any limitations at all. We have broader opportunities today than I had in the very beginning. So I'm looking forward to a continuing, productive career.

Alejandro Zaffaroni, Founder of Alza and Syntex

It's very likely that the jack-of-all-trades would learn from his or her experiences and go on to success. Like the great restaurant entrepreneur who had a lemonade stand in a bad location before opening an award-winning eatery. Or the legendary high-tech CEO who, at his previous company, hired a staff of people with their own agendas—agendas that weren't the same as his company vision. Just about every successful entrepreneur in Silicon Valley has experienced failure—some small and some colossal. Entrepreneurs are human—but entrepreneurs in Silicon Valley live in a community that accepts failure for what it is: an experiment. Just as in the science lab, where multiple failures may occur but the experiments still provide critical information on the road to ultimate success, so too can "failure" in business result in increases in knowledge and future triumphs.

Varian's two early core technologies were displayed in a 1953 trade show.

"I did my thesis at Berkeley. I ended up with ten to twenty patents that were in a new phenomenon and one thing I did was go to Hewlett-Packard and see if they would like to buy them.

Dave Packard said, 'Well, I tell you, I'll make you a deal. For the first six months everything you can write down will be your part of that deal and after that they're ours.'

Very pragmatic. He won me over right then.

But as I was leaving I was talking to the research director and said, 'I'm assuming that Hewlett-Packard will go into digital techniques for their instrumentation and likely digital processing on the computers.'

'Not a chance,' he replied.

So that whole thing fell through right then. Part of history."

**Doug Engelbart, Visionary,
Inventor of the Computer Mouse**

Johannes Gensfleis... Gutenberg was born ... Mainz, Germany, ... 1397.

In 1452, with the aid ... borrowed mone... Gutenberg began h... bible project. Tw... hundred copies of t... two-volume Gutenbe... Bible were printed, ... small number (possib... as many as 50) of whi... were printed on vellu... The expensive ar... exquisite bibles we... completed and sold at t... 1455 Frankfurt Bo... Fair. Roughly a quart... of all the Gutenbe... Bibles survive today...

In 1455, Gutenbe... lost his press to h... investor, Johann Fu... but Gutenberg invent... other mainstays ... traditional printing. I... ink, a mixture of o... copper, and lea... remains bright over 5... years later. Gutenbe... died in 1468.

THE COMPUTER: AT THE CORE OF COMMUNICATION

While some think that the abacus may have been the first computing device, which long-ago merchants used to keep track of their transactions, others look at the invention of the printing press, in 1438, as a precursor to the Industrial Age and the wonders of the machine. Johann Gutenberg's printing of the Mazarin Bible, with movable type, ink, press, and paper, first made information available in both quantity and quality. It also set the stage for the computer,

The Difference Engine (which preceded the Analytical Engine) was designed by Charles Babbage in the 1800s. Unfortunately, the technology of the time didn't allow its complete construction.

I n ninth grade, I stumbled onto what makes a computer do more than just a calculator. A computer can analyze and analyze and analyze and loop and repeat and execute lots of little statements. That concept hit me in ninth grade when I saw someone else's science fair project. By the end of high school, that was my life. I was ordering every computer manual I could from every company that made computers. Then I was ordering chip manuals from the local companies that made chips because I understood how to design with chips. I had taught myself.

**Steve Wozniak,
Founder of Apple**

centuries later in the Information Age, to once again revolutionize communication by bringing together science, design, and the ability to process information.

The first computers were actually more like calculators than printing presses. Charles Babbage, a British math professor in the early 1800s, became frustrated by the many mistakes he found while studying calculations made for the Royal Astronomical Society. He came up with the idea for a mechanical calculating machine driven by an external set of instructions to perform basic mathematical calculations and print the results. The machine, which was designed to be powered by steam and was as big as a train engine, eventually led to Babbage's Analytical Engine, the first general-purpose computer—which,

Charles Babbage

I n two years time we will start seeing wearable computers of the same scale as the laptop being carried around without the need to have a bulky briefcase or some big gadget that you're obviously carrying. You can discreetly tuck it away. And in five years time these things will have all disappeared into our clothing though perhaps not sewn into the clothing because they might, after all, be expensive or have valuable data. There are things that you can easily slip into your pocket and just forget about in the same way that you probably put your pants on with your wallet in the pocket, if you're anything like me.

**Vaughn Pratt,
Founder of Sun Microsystems**

though similar in concept to the modern computer, was never built in workable form.

Involved with Babbage's Analytical Engine was one of the first women of computers, Augusta Ada King. The daughter of the English poet Lord Byron, Ada King, who later became the Countess of Lovelace, was one of the few people who understood Babbage's design as well as Babbage himself. King helped to secure funding from the British government for building the Engine and translated an article from the French about the machine's development and specifics. She also suggested to Babbage that he write a plan for how the Analytical Engine might calculate Bernoulli numbers, a plan that is now thought of as the first computer program. King correctly theorized, in her 1843 article, that a computer like the Analytical Engine would some day be used to compose complex music, produce graphics, and be used for practical as well as scientific purposes. In honor of Ada King, a software language developed by the U.S. Department of Defense in 1979 was named "Ada."

More than a hundred years after the attempt to build a working Analytical Engine, driven by the Allied defense needs of World War II, giant steps in computer construction were finally achieved. In England, a series of electronic machines named Colossus were built and used to decipher German coded intelligence messages. In the U.S., in 1945, a computer known as the ENIAC (electronic numerical integrator and computer) was built at the Ballistic Research Laboratory in Aberdeen, Maryland, a 30-ton programmable, decimal-based machine with several specialized processing units.

Following the war, in 1946, the developers of the ENIAC, John Mauchly and J. Presper Eckert, formed what is thought to be the first computer company, the Electronic Controls Company, to design a new computer system and identify the electronic computer's uses. The company's first client was the U.S. Census Bureau, in need of a large-scale computer to handle the huge amounts of data that would be involved with the upcoming 1950 census. Since manufacturers and government policy makers were in need of timely information about postwar economic recovery efforts, the Census Bureau was also interested in the electronic computer's speed. But while Mauchly and Eckert were able to develop an experimental model in their lab, they were never able to produce a commercial system, and sold their company to Remington Rand in 1950. Rand went on to develop and deliver the UNIVAC, an electronic computer designed specifically for data processing

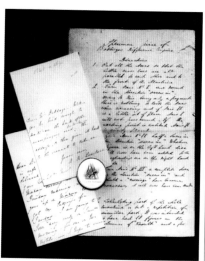

Augusta Ada King, Lady Lovelace, was one of the most picturesque characters in computer history.

and one that could add 100,000 10-digit numbers per second.

Through the '50s and '60s, progress in the computer world continued, driven in great part by the transformative invention of the transistor and later the integrated circuit. In the early '60s, Douglas Engelbart, a scientist at Stanford Research Institute, pursued his mission to find ways to augment human intelligence and solve ever more complex problems by developing computer aids such as the mouse and hypertext. To meet the needs of the new machines that were constantly being developed, high-order languages, including FORTRAN and COBOL, were created by other scientists and developers. Computer size decreased while power, capability, and speed increased dramatically.

Then, in 1974, *Radio-Electronics* magazine published an article about the construction of the "personal computer," a desk-sized machine equipped with the system, software, and memory for completing multiple information-processing tasks. The Altair 8800 was introduced in kit form, followed by the revolutionary Apple II, the first assembled computer successfully introduced into the mainstream. Software became much more important, and customized applications began to proliferate.

Two views of the UNIVAC, the first commercial computer, which was installed at the United States Bureau of the Census in 1951

During the 1980s, the price of computing dropped dramatically, making it possible for many more people to reap the enormous benefits. The old JCL (job control language) was replaced by the user-friendly GUI (graphical user interface). In the '90s, laptops and handheld computers moved to center stage, along with wireless computing and the Internet.

Though a '90s phenomenon, the Internet actually began when the U.S. collaboration of educational and research institutions called the Advanced Research Projects Agency, or ARPA, created packet-switching technology—a way to divide data into tiny packets of information that could take different routes along a network to reach their destination. First designed for military use, to provide security during the transfer of critical information, packet-switching technology and the ARPA network known as ARPANET were the

---

We used a simple, very elegant piece of mathematics by a mathematician called Pierre Baisier to describe the outlines of characters and the curves of those outlines. The trick was to get those to convert to bits, to the individual dots, in a way in which the character wasn't, in some sense, distorted by what is called aliasing, by shifting the staffs around. We came up with a very elegant solution that was not thought possible at that time, that enabled the printing solution to solve all kinds of problems, and that, along with the focus on an open architecture and an open standard, opening it up rather than keeping it proprietary, caused the early success of desktop publishing and, ultimately, changed the whole world of printing and publishing.

John Warnock, Founder of Adobe

beginnings of the huge system of linked computers we know today as the Internet.

But you could also say that the Internet began long before ARPA developed its revolutionary concept, and even before J.C.R. Licklider of the Massachusetts Institute of Technology wrote of his "galactic network" concept in 1962. The Internet truly got its start in the 1800s, with the laying of transatlantic cable, the creation of the telegraph and the telephone, and the development of canal and railway systems that networked every part of America, enabling people to communicate much more quickly and

---

A young Steve Jobs promoting Apple's newest product: the Apple II. "It was real neat in the popular media to express this idea of two kids coming from nowhere."

–Steve Wozniak

easily. We can really think of the Internet as simply the newest, albeit the most advanced, medium for linking people, goods, and services and promoting the exchange of information.

Just like its predecessors, and with its worldwide capabilities, the Internet has revolutionized communication. With just a computer and online access, individuals in every reach of the world can conduct business, bank, study and learn, invest, collaborate, shop, enjoy music and art, and write to each other with no thought for geography. The Internet and the World Wide Web have had a profound and continuing effect

---

on nearly every aspect of our lives and are taking us from an industrial economy to an economy based on knowledge.

One of the most important ways the Internet has enhanced our knowledge is through providing opportunities to learn about other cultures. With just a few clicks of the mouse, information on history, art, music, customs, government, and daily life is available regarding just about any nation or group of people. Even books and other sources of information written in foreign languages can be quickly translated for the non-native speaker, widening our understanding of what's well outside our immediate domain. This ability to learn about and understand the lives and ways of others, and about the world we co-inhabit, can serve to link us more tightly as our society and the Internet continue to grow and change.

But though the Internet is certainly a driving force of our time, the invention of the computer, according to some, may be the most important event in the history of technology—if not the most important in history itself. While the point can be argued, it is certainly true that, like the printing press before it, the computer has fomented change throughout society and has had enormously far-reaching effects. As the future unfolds, it is likely that computers will become even more ubiquitous as they continue to grow in power and capability and as they become embedded to work invisibly in new products and in new ways. And it is very likely that Silicon Valley technology will continue to be a great source behind that growth.

Steven Wozniak

Steven Wozniak, the Woz, is a Silicon Valley native. His father worked as an engineer at Lockheed Missiles and Space Company. Woz attended Homestead High School in Cupertino, where he excelled at science projects and athletics. If any one scientist can be credited with bringing the personal computer into the homes of the world, it would be Woz.

Shy, socially conscious, a big, gentle man, Steven Wozniak is a founder of Apple. His passion from an early age was to make an electrical device work with fewer parts.

"I used to design computers and tried to redesign them with fewer chips. I would find another chip that would make it smaller. I eventually wound up (if I was trying to solve a circuit that did one thing like generate some timing signal) looking through the manual at other chips that weren't designed to do that. They were designed to do other things. But, if the logic of the chip worked out right and it did generate the timing signals doing something else, great."

Steven Wozniak

Every two weeks we had a meeting at the Stanford Linear Accelerator Center, on Wednesday nights, and boy, that was the most important day of my life. The rest of the two weeks all my spare time was spent planning and writing some software to show up… At this event, the Home Brew Computer Club, I'd go down there, and as shy as I was, I'd never raise my hand and say anything. There was a period where we could show off something we had, and I'd set up my computer with my Sears color TV. People would come up and ask questions, and I could answer them. And that was kind of what the start was like. It was just an atmosphere. There were no companies yet that were big, but there were a bunch of companies that had names that were well known. There were about three magazines that started up, and they spread the word nationally, so we all took ads. Apple Computer took ads in the early Byte magazines. And so we were known by hundreds of thousands of people, even though we only sold 100 computers."

Steven Wozniak
Founder of Apple

I can remember Steve and Steve [Wozniak and Jobs] working on the product Breakout, and doing a design that was so clever, because in those days it was heavily hardware, they essentially broke the bank. We felt that 70 chips were about normal and that if you could get it down to 60 you were really doing well. I think they got it down to 38. The only problem was it used so many feedback loops that you couldn't really test it. So we had to escalate it back up again. But, they got the bonus and everybody was happy.

Nolan Bushnell,
Founder of Atari

There's something marvelous about Steve Wozniak. He brings out the protective nature in people because he has an innocence about him… on the whole, he is as pure an inventor as you're going to find in this town.

Mike Malone,
Editor of *Forbes ASAP*

OUR FOUNDER

INKTOMI CORPORATION

www.inktomi.com

Full-length books. Department store catalogs. Product information. Reviews and guides. Even audio and video files. So much is available through the Internet these days, but accessing just the information you want just when you want it can be hard—especially as the amount of data and the number of Internet users grow.

Inktomi Corporation develops and markets Internet infrastructure software that lets Internet users find and access information quickly and easily, and helps speed the flow of traffic, including rich media content, across networks. When the company was founded by University of California at Berkeley research scientists Eric Brewer and Paul Gauthier, in 1996, its first application was a prototype search engine that could sift through large amounts of data without the use of expensive supercomputers. Now the award-winning company offers a wide range of networking products as well as search and commerce software solutions. Inktomi is based in Foster City, California, and has offices throughout North America, Asia, and Europe.

Inktomi's flexible, scalable software is based on patented core technology that links multiple workstations through high-speed connections to function as one extremely powerful computer. The technology also supports thousands of operations per processor, and uses advanced algorithms to automatically identify and categorize Web pages

according to specific classification schemes. Inktomi's technology forms the foundation of a powerful Internet software layer for some of the largest search engines, comparison shopping sites, and service provider networks in the world, including America Online, AT&T, Excite@Home, Genuity, iWon, KPNQwest, and MSN.

Inktomi's founding application, now known as Inktomi Search Solutions, encompasses a wide range of hosted services and licensed software serving the search needs of leading portals, destination sites, and enterprise intranets and extranets. Inktomi Search/Web is the world's most popular search engine, providing portals and destination sites with a customizable, private-label solution. With six geographically distributed search clusters on four continents, local support services, and years of experience maintaining the highest level of operational excellence, Inktomi is uniquely prepared to meet the needs of international Web site search services. In addition, Inktomi's software enables its customers to offer a variety of services, which include creating and maintaining complex Web directories and leveraging online commerce and merchandising capabilities.

Another Inktomi search solution is Inktomi Search/Custom, for public Web sites that provide search and navigation capabilities for selected subsets of the Web. Two other search solutions are Inktomi Search/Site, for dot-com destination sites and corporate Web sites; and Inktomi Search/Enterprise, for intranets,

Image from the Mind advertisement in Inktomi's 2000 ad campaign: "Mind, essential to you Inktomi, essential to the Internet."

extranets, educational institutions, and government organizations. Inktomi's licensed Search Software solutions for custom, enterprise, and site requirements provide natural-language search capabilities in an easy-to-install, easy-to-run downloadable package, and are currently used by more than 2,000 organizations worldwide.

Inktomi also provides an essential commerce infrastructure for a wide range of portals, vertical portals, destination sites, merchants, devices, and applications.

Inktomi Commerce Engine software is the first platform to incorporate all parts of the shopping process, including researching a product category, comparing prices, and buying. The Commerce Engine gives users access to such information as reviews from *Consumers Digest* and user commentary from *Delphi* to help them make informed purchasing decisions. Inktomi plans to integrate its Search Engine and Commerce Engine software to provide Web sites with a sophisticated, private-label shopping product that will be the most comprehensive, scalable product yet. Customers such as American Express and iWon.com currently use Inktomi Commerce Engine software to extend the reach of their e-commerce services. The Commerce Engine provides access to hundreds of merchants and millions of products, and integrates with "electronic wallets." It also provides the needed infrastructure for billing, reporting, data mining, tracking, and traffic analysis.

To speed the flow of information once it's located, Inktomi offers a range of products that provide a seamless network software layer for the Internet. Inktomi Network Products deliver the infrastructure for the reliable distribution, delivery, and management of content and applications across large, complex service provider and enterprise networks deployed within many of the world's leading corporations.

Inktomi Traffic Server is the industry's first large-scale commercial network cache, a software-based data storage and access platform that increases network efficiency while reducing congestion over the Internet. The software is the only product currently available that is designed to handle more than a terabyte (a trillion bytes) of data, making it the world's highest-performing cache. Traffic Server speeds up data retrieval time and cuts down on traffic by storing temporary copies of frequently accessed information closer to users, at the edges of a network, which makes users' online time much easier and much more rewarding. America Online, whose caches receive more than 7 billion hits each day, uses Traffic Server to speed and manage its network traffic.

The real power of Traffic Server, however, is its "platform" functionality. This functionality supports dozens of third-party software applications through an open application programming interface (API), making it a virtual operating system for the Internet. For example, a network filtering system that works with the Traffic Server platform enables customers to block access to certain kinds of Internet content, such as adult materials. Content transformation extensions that are deployed on top of Traffic Server translate content so that it can be delivered to wireless Internet devices such as Web-enabled cellular phones. Broadband extensions enable service providers to distribute on-demand applications faster and more efficiently to customers around the world. In addition, leading information technology

One of Inktomi's computer clusters that powers the Inktomi Search Engine

(IT) providers such as Intel and 3Com have licensed an original equipment manufacturer (OEM) version of Traffic Server to incorporate in current and future hardware caching appliances.

Another Inktomi first is Content Delivery Suite, an integrated software solution for content distribution, delivery, and management. When used with Inktomi Traffic Server, Content Delivery Suite synchronizes the delivery of information to globally distributed servers and caches, making content delivery more cost effective and efficient. Content Delivery Suite works directly to help service providers and enterprises accomplish their goal of delivering the right information to the right user at the right time.

Inktomi also provides a complete range of solutions for distributing rich media content on the Internet. Optimized for on-demand delivery, Traffic Server Media IXT is a streaming media cache that stores media files and distributes them in a way that provides the highest-quality experience possible, given various Internet connection speeds. Inktomi also offers a complete framework for broadcasting and managing the distribution of "live" content (events or pre-recorded mass-distributed programs) on the Internet. This software technology platform allows service providers and enterprises to deliver highly scalable, reliable, and manageable broadcast services, using their existing infrastructure, that support millions of viewers and thousands of simultaneous media broadcasts.

Inktomi also provides a wireless platform optimized for the predicted explosion in the growth of the wireless Internet. This platform is designed to handle increasing numbers of users and amounts of data; provide wireless subscribers with highly relevant, differentiated content and commerce services; and manage multiple capabilities, including content and application delivery, billing, provisioning, and transformation. Inktomi's wireless capabilities are focused on delivering revenue-generating mobile services for wireless operators while providing millions of wireless subscribers worldwide with highly relevant, differentiated content and commerce services.

In just a few years, Inktomi has grown from an idea for a research project to a global enterprise whose products are core to the Internet infrastructure. In fact, with its rapid climb to its current position of leadership, you could say that the company has already lived up to the fame of the spider it was named for—a spider found in Lakota Indian lore that was known for his ability to defeat larger adversaries through his wit and cunning. Under the leadership of CEO David Peterschmidt, this fast-moving company is expected to grow along with the Internet as more users go online and even more information becomes available. Inktomi's mission is to add to the "software fabric" at the foundation of the Internet in order to provide users with improved service, increase customer profitability by optimizing their bandwidth investment, and deliver new and ever-better network services.

HEWLETT-PACKARD COMPANY

www.hp.com

It seems that nearly everyone on the planet knows the story of how Bill Hewlett and Dave Packard started a tiny electronics business in 1939 in a garage in Palo Alto, California. Most people also likely know that since that time, Hewlett-Packard has followed the "HP Way"—a way of doing business based on quality, performance, and respect—to become a world leader in computer systems, imaging, printing, and information technology services. At the end of the last century, Hewlett-Packard employed 86,000 people and had revenues of over $42 billion.

But the turn of the millennium brought big changes to HP. The company's test and measurement business was spun off to become an independent company called Agilent Technologies. Long-time president and CEO Lew Platt retired and leadership was taken over

Carly Fiorina, Hewlett-Packard chairman and CEO

by Carly Fiorina. And the company decided to capitalize on the wealth of opportunities resulting from the growth of the Internet and go "back to the garage" and reinvent itself.

After examining the company's strengths, management realized that they could position HP at the meeting point of Internet services, appliances, and infrastructure. They launched what they called their e-services strategy, focused on transforming the Internet into an information utility that would work for people in numerous beneficial ways invisibly. The company has since created, in partnership with other companies, Internet "applications on tap," industry-specific trading communities, and networks of service providers that address particular business processes, such as accounting. They have also introduced an Internet software platform called e-speak. This interactive technology makes it possible to create, request, and locate services on the Internet from any electronic device. And, because so much business is done on the Internet now, HP also launched a new way to handle data storage—scalable networked storage. This architecture supports a wide array of storage devices and provides 100% data availability for the mountains of data e-services generate.

To make it easier for people to do business over the Internet, Hewlett-Packard added high-speed processors to their workstations, corporate PCs, and home PCs. They also introduced a line of computers for small and medium-size businesses, making available a complete e-commerce solution for under $500 and

Two Stanford University graduates, Dave Packard and Bill Hewlett, founded Hewlett-Packard Company in 1939 in this Palo Alto, California, garage. The structure is a California State Historical Landmark.

making HP a leader in business-to-business technologies and solutions. A new server for small businesses incorporated free disaster-recovery software. HP's high-end UNIX servers were engineered for large-scale applications and databases, and now serve as a computer engine that meets or exceeds the needs of enterprise customers. And, to expand the capabilities of home-based computer users, HP combined its CD Writer with a line of PCs, and made it possible for consumers to order PCs directly from the company's Web site. For mobile computing, a line of HP notebooks now provides easy access to the Internet and a number of multimedia tools, for both business and consumer customers. The company's palm-sized PC boasts a color screen and 12-hour

battery life.

When Hewlett-Packard introduced its first thermal inkjet printer in the mid-1980s, printing was revolutionized. It also pioneered LaserJet technology, and has sold more than 50 million LaserJet printers, enough to extend from San Francisco to Tokyo and back again. The company also offers a complete line of cutting-edge scanners, copiers, fax machines, imaging services, and digital photography products to make printing and imaging even more extraordinary. HP's enterprise software helps customers use and share imaging information from a variety of sources and deliver it to multiple output devices in the right format. Imaging services are provided to consumers through an HP Web site that allows the sharing of images around the world.

While many things have changed at HP, its commitment to making a contribution to society as well as to technology has not. The company supports such educational and charitable organizations as the Institute for Women and Technology, the United Nations High Commission on Refugees, and the Hispanic Student Outreach Program. Employees are also working to advance communication through such research projects as CoolTown, in which people, places, and things are networked together through the Web. Work is also in full swing at HP Laboratories, where researchers are looking for alternatives to silicon chip technology. Hewlett-Packard is not only reinventing itself, it is reinventing how people live and work together.

AVAYA

www.avaya.com

Avaya specializes in feature-rich telephone sets developed for productivity and customer satisfaction.

Avaya is all about communication. Not just talking or exchanging data or images, but connecting with every person and every piece of information that's needed. Though a company whose name is new to the business world, Avaya is on a mission to help businesses communicate in a better way.

Headquartered in Basking Ridge, New Jersey, Avaya has 30,000 employees and is led by president and CEO Donald K. Peterson. In its first year the company became a leader in the sales of messaging systems, cabling systems, enterprise voice communication systems, and call center systems. The 500 employees who make up Avaya's Communications Applications Group, which is based in Milpitas, California, focus on messaging solutions, customer care systems, and Internet solutions.

Avaya concentrates on providing high-performance communication solutions to enterprises operating in the fast-changing environment of e-business.

The company offers voice, converged voice and data, customer relationship management, messaging, networking, and cabling products and services, so that businesses have the resources necessary to let them communicate directly, clearly, and quickly with employees, customers, and partners. Avaya's solutions work to break down barriers among networks, systems, and devices—in other words, to communicate without boundaries.

The hardware and software Avaya provides are concentrated in four main areas. The company's customer relationship management (CRM) software applications help businesses connect with their customers. Avaya provides multimedia customer care and computer telephony applications, CRM software, dialing products, and interactive voice response products. The company's unified communications and portal software applications integrate messaging, video conferencing, Web collaboration, and portal technologies to enable businesses to communicate more completely and at a lower cost.

A third key area in which Avaya provides cutting-edge communication products and services is hosted solutions for application service providers (ASPs). Because of the growing complexity of handling e-business applications, many organizations are outsourcing this work to xSPs, or next-generation service providers. Avaya's hosted solutions for service providers are prepackaged, integrated combinations of Avaya hardware and software that give employees, customers, partners, suppliers, and distributors access to the information they need, regardless of their location. These products streamline business processes and link everyone involved to the "virtual enterprise."

Multiservice infrastructure products are Avaya's fourth main group of communication solutions. These products are advanced platforms on which Avaya's software applications run. The company's structured cabling system gives customers a state-of-the-art physical infrastructure, which enables streamlined voice and data communication over multiple data transfer standards, including Internet Protocol (IP), Asynchronous Transfer Mode (ATM), and Time Division Multiplexing (TDM).

In addition to its many products, Avaya offers its customers a full range of services and support, including planning and consulting, installing and integration, and support and maintenance. The company's global service organization also provides remote diagnostic testing, monitoring, and problem resolution. Professional services for customer and enterprise relationship management are another Avaya plus.

The company's research and development laboratory, Avaya Labs, is composed of more than 3,000 R&D professionals who are focused on creating new and better business communication applications, CRM innovations, messaging solutions, and new business infrastructures. These scientists have experience and expertise in the areas of data analysis, multimedia technology, networked applications, software development, and information management. The laboratory has branches in California, New Jersey, Texas, and other U.S. states, as well as in the United Kingdom, Australia, Israel, and Canada.

Avaya has helped more than one million business customers in more than 90 countries improve their business communications. The company's innovative technology, R&D program, and customer support have made it a choice of more than 75% of the Fortune 500 companies. While Avaya continues to work toward fulfilling its corporate mission, it has already been named number one worldwide in the sales of automatic call distribution systems and interactive voice response systems for call centers. It is also number one worldwide in sales of connectivity products for enterprise networks and number one in the U.S. for sales of voice communication systems.

ORACLE CORPORATION

www.oracle.com

As increasing numbers of companies are transforming themselves into e-businesses and using the Internet to replace old, expensive ways of managing operations, they are turning to Oracle Corporation for integrated, Internet-enabled software.

Oracle Corporation, headquartered in Redwood Shores, California, is the first software company to develop and deploy 100% Internet-enabled enterprise

Larry Ellison has been the CEO of Oracle Corporation since he founded the company in 1977.

software across its entire product line: database, application server, the E-Business Suite of enterprise business applications, and application development and decision support tools. Founded in 1977, and led by chairman and CEO Lawrence J. Ellison, the company offers a wide range of e-business products that provide a cost-effective way for customers to expand their market opportunities and make their operations more efficient. Oracle software runs on network computers, PCs, workstations, minicomputers, mainframes, personal digital assistants, and set-top boxes.

In October 2000, Oracle introduced Oracle9i™, which consists of the Oracle9i Database and the Oracle9i Application Server. Oracle9i is the only software infrastructure needed to support today's e-business applications and the Internet's next generation of collaborative applications. The Oracle9i Application Server makes it possible for organizations to access data on any server, over any network, from any device. Its caching, or content delivery, technology provides greater performance and reliability. The Oracle9i Application Server increases Web site performance and has built-in reporting and query capabilities. The company guarantees that this software will run a Web site three times faster than comparable software.

The Oracle9i Database also enables businesses and organizations to access any data on any server, over any network, from any client device, and is designed for the emerging hosted application market on the Internet. Oracle9i Real Application Clusters, a

key option of the Oracle9i Database, allows customers to support an unlimited number of online users and an unlimited amount of data. Considered by many as the "holy grail," this software runs any purchased application unchanged on a computer cluster.

Another breakthrough product, the Oracle® E-Business Suite, is award-winning software designed to take full advantage of the Internet. This complete e-business product lets customers put every aspect of their business operation on the Internet, and prevents them from having to buy different applications from different suppliers, only to find they don't work together. The integrated product provides enterprise-wide information so that customers get a complete view of their business, including customers, partners, and suppliers. Oracle E-Business Suite is available in 29 languages and supports local business practices and legal requirements. It is the first set of applications that works with a single global database.

In addition to the many high-performing software products Oracle delivers, the company also offers comprehensive consulting, education, and support services. Oracle Consulting helps customers use Oracle software in ways that will meet their particular needs, from data warehousing to customer relationship management to e-commerce. Using their technical expertise and industry knowledge, and the company's innovative technology, consultants work with clients to build a complete business solution that harnesses the power of the Internet. Oracle Support Services

employs more than 6,600 professionals to provide local-language software support to customers 24 hours a day. Oracle Education offers technology training to customers and partners in more than 70 countries.

Because not everyone is able to share in the benefits technology brings, Oracle has developed several programs to help improve the quality of life in its communities. Oracle Volunteers gives employees the opportunity to volunteer their time and talent to help with local projects such as food drives and teaching math and business skills to school-aged children. Oracle's Corporate Giving program funds, partners with, and makes grants to nonprofit organizations and schools to support advancement in such fields as education and medical research. The Oracle Promise program donates computers to public schools to make digital access a reality for all children, and is working to make it possible for every child in America to have access to a computer and the Internet.

Oracle's world headquarters located in Redwood Shores, California

CISCO SYSTEMS

www.cisco.com

For many years, Cisco Systems Inc. has been a powerful force behind the momentum of the Internet. The company's leadership has consistently focused on the concept that the Internet will someday connect everyone and everything—and that Cisco's networking products and services can help to bring that day about. John Chambers, Cisco's president and CEO, holds that, in the future, everyone will be able to access the Internet wherever they are and whenever they want. People all over the world will be able to send and receive the information they need.

Cisco has been driving the growth of the Internet by providing a huge range of hardware products that form information networks and give people access to those networks. Their hardware products allow small groups as well as global enterprises to build a common information infrastructure even though users may work on different types of computers. In addition, Cisco software enables networked applications, such as electronic business transactions and distance learning.

Like the Internet itself, Cisco Systems, now headquartered in San Jose, California, originally grew out of the need to communicate. In the early 1980s, two computer systems managers at Stanford University were frustrated by not being able to link and share their separate departments' computer networks. Working with several graduate students, they developed the router, the key to connectivity. Twenty years later, their solution and the company they co-founded have resulted in a multinational corporation with more than 30,000 employees. The company is now the worldwide leader in networking products for the Internet, with over $12 billion in revenues.

The products the company offers fall under several categories. One major category is routers, the descendants of the company's first product. Cisco's powerful routers are small devices that move information from one network to another while making sure that the information reaches its destination quickly and safely.

Another product category is switches. Switching is important because it controls where information is routed. Cisco's switches are circuits used in both local-area network (LAN) and wide-area network (WAN) communication.

A third group of Cisco products lets people communicate by computer from home, a remote office, or while traveling. The company's ISDN (Integrated Services Digital Network) routers are helping this new communication technology to transmit voice, data, music, and video in digital form. Their dial-up access servers, DSL (Digital Subscriber Line) technologies, and cable broadband routers give mobile workers and telecommuters Internet access, and a powerful link to the information and people they need to reach.

Once online, network users need to be certain that the information they send and receive is secure. Cisco has special Internet products that prevent unauthorized access to a network. Other Internet solutions scan networks for security risks and detect and respond to unauthorized network activity. Still other products enable quick network access and eliminate redundant content.

Because Cisco's management and staff are so knowledgeable about networking, they work with other companies to help them set up networking infrastructures to reap the benefits online applications can bring. Cisco's Internet Business Solutions Group consults on effective Internet business practices. And its Cisco Resource Network provides information and tools to help small businesses learn about the Internet. The Resource Network also assists with network installation and support.

Beyond effecting business solutions, the Internet is also playing a part in the way people live. Because Cisco's leaders recognize the importance of this global reach, they are actively participating in programs to improve people's lives. On the education front, the company has formed an alliance called the Cisco Networking Academy Program, which helps students prepare for the networking jobs of the future. Cisco's work with the United Nations Development Program is mobilizing people around the world to use the Web as an information source to end poverty. The company also meets with heads of state to discuss how the Internet can improve national economies.

As the Internet and business networks grow and change, new and exciting opportunities are opening up for people and companies around the world. To help them take advantage of these opportunities, Cisco will continue to empower the Internet generation by designing, providing, and supporting the systems that make networking work.

Cisco founders Sandy Lerner and Leonard Bosack

ADOBE SYSTEMS

www.adobe.com

Helping people communicate. That's been the goal of Adobe Systems since it first produced the software that touched off the desktop publishing revolution. Since that time, in 1982, the company has continued to create ever more powerful and beneficial software to meet a wide range of printing and publishing needs.

Adobe Systems was founded by two research scientists, John Warnock and Chuck Geschke, who jointly directed the company's growth until 2000, when Geschke retired. Warnock retired in 2001. The pair's first product was the software application PostScript®, which is still the industry standard. PostScript incorporates a page-description language that transmits even the most complex page of text and graphics from computer to corporate or personal printer. A new PostScript product enables digital printing on corporate networks, the Internet, and digital document distribution systems.

Because Adobe's market includes professional publishers, Web publishers, business publishers, and individual consumers, it provides a large number of products for creating and distributing information. These are grouped under four principal business units—Web Publishing, Print Publishing, ePaper Solutions, and OEM PostScript, or software and technology based on the PostScript standard. One of the company's products, Adobe Photoshop®, is the dominant software program used

for computer editing of photographs and graphics. And company statistics indicate that the majority of images on the Web have been created or modified with one or more Adobe products.

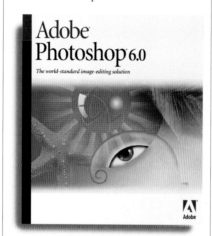

Adobe Photoshop® is the dominant software program used for computer editing of photographs and graphics.

With the explosion of the Internet, a new world of online communication has come into existence. To take part in this world, businesses everywhere need design and management tools that allow them to present—easily, accurately, and compellingly—their products and services over the Web. Software is also needed that allows consumers to see and understand what is being offered. Adobe's Web publishing products meet these needs by enabling graphics, video, digital-photograph images, animation, navigational buttons, and banners to be included on Web pages. For example, one of their products lets Web authors design, lay out, and produce cutting-edge Web sites without complicated multimedia programming. Another

lets users import, edit, and send photos in e-mails.

While Internet communication has increased rapidly, neither it, nor TV nor the radio, has ended communicating on paper. In fact, the great success of the Internet has actually depended heavily on printed advertising, billboards, and direct mail. Many of Adobe's applications are used to create much of the printed materials people read every day, including magazines, newspapers, catalogs, and reports. One product, called Adobe InDesign™, is a page-layout application for graphics professionals based on a new object-oriented architecture. One of Adobe's packages of fonts provides more than 2,500 different printing typefaces. And its Framemaker® products enable authoring and publishing of lengthy documents, including books and technical manuals. An early product, Adobe Illustrator®, has been a leading illustration tool for creating artwork for printed materials. Its latest generation now creates artwork for the Web.

What Adobe calls its ePaper Solutions include software that combines paper and digital publishing capabilities. Adobe Acrobat® may be the most widely known product in this category. Acrobat lets users easily convert a computer file from another application to a PDF, or Portable Document Format. This cross-platform electronic format keeps the layout, colors, and artwork of the original file but allows them to be distributed and viewed through a Web browser. The Reader part of Acrobat can be downloaded free from Adobe's Web site to let users view and

print PDF files.

Adobe's original printing technology, PostScript, has grown along with the company. Graphics professionals and publishers use it now to produce state-of-the-art printed and digital documents for today's sophisticated public. A recent version of PostScript provides the technology for print on demand and high-resolution image setting. Another printing product allows low-cost, high-quality printing for home and small office use.

From its small beginnings, San Jose, California's Adobe Systems has grown into the third-largest U.S.–based personal software company. But current CEO Bruce Chizen says its original mission—to help people communicate—will continue to drive its momentum. Adobe leaders predict that their products and services will go on enabling people to spend less time learning how to use technology and more time using it to communicate creatively.

CEO Bruce Chizen (left) standing with Adobe founder John Warnock

QUANTUM CORPORATION

www.quantum.com

With the huge increase in Internet use and the need for computer networking systems with a worldwide reach, the requirements for managing and transferring digital data have also skyrocketed. As part of those requirements, computer users, from at-home Internet surfers to corporate Information Technology managers, are demanding higher capacity and higher performance from the products that store digital content. These hard disk drive devices store data on multiple rotating magnetic disks and allow users to access the information at a moment's notice.

Quantum Corporation, based in Milpitas, California, offers many data storage solutions for use in the home, the home office, small businesses, and large corporate enterprises. The company has become the world's leading storage supplier in six of the seven markets it serves. Its products include hard disk drives for the PC and consumer electronics, tape drives, and network-attached storage (NAS) appliances. In fact, it supplies more than half the drives that Apple Computer uses in its products. Quantum's high-end, high-capacity hard drives provide fast data access for use with graphics, desktop publishing, multimedia, and server applications.

Along with the increase in Internet use, there's also been a great increase in the numbers of consumer electronic devices. Because of the interest in these products, a new platform has been created for the common disk drive. Quantum now designs and develops for this platform. Its drives can be found in such devices as the PVR (personal video recorder) and the audio jukebox. One of its hard drive products, Quantum QuickView™, lets TV watchers freeze, fast-forward, and rewind live television programs. This allows viewers to watch their favorite shows on their own schedule. In the future, Quantum hard disk drives also will be found in many other high-performance consumer applications, such as game consoles. The freedom hard drives bring to storage and access time will enable game developers to produce increasingly dynamic and feature-rich products for consumers to enjoy.

For corporate customers, Quantum produces DLTtape™ drives, media cartridges, and tape libraries that back up large amounts of data stored on network servers. Such servers allow computer users in any size organization to share applications and data from a central location. Storing information on tape is the least expensive way to keep large quantities of digital content, because tape provides a larger storage surface area than other devices. Quantum's half-inch tape technology provides a greater recording area than other solutions. It also requires shorter periods of time to back up and archive information stored on hard disk drives.

In addition to tape storage equipment, Quantum also develops Snap Servers™. These are network-attached storage systems designed to meet the great new storage requirements resulting from the increased use of the Internet. Snap Servers provide fast access to data for multimedia applications such as digital video and audio streaming, as well as animation. Plug-and-play Snap Servers are

"Take Your Kids to Work Day," April 1998

independent of servers, and plug directly into a network. Designed with today's high-speed business environments in mind, they work with a variety of networking platforms, including Windows NT, UNIX, and Mac.

Another area in which Quantum also leads is the solid-state disk (SSD) market. These disks store massive amounts of data in random access memory (RAM) rather than magnetically. Quantum's SSDs have the high-execution speeds needed for computer imaging, multimedia, video-on-demand, processing of on-line transactions, and scientific modeling.

As life continues to move at Internet speed, Chairman and CEO Michael Brown believes that the demand for new and ever-better solutions for managing digital content will grow. In fact, it is estimated that worldwide storage needs are already increasing at a rate of 100% to 150% every year. Quantum aims to remain at the forefront of meeting this challenge, offering greater storage capacity and innovative products to address the needs of Internet, communications, and multimedia applications.

The Deep Extragalactic Evolutionary Probe (DEEP) 136 Quantum Atlas II hard drives are in use to collect and analyze deep space information that has been collected by the Hubble space telescope.

FUJITSU SOFTWARE CORPORATION

www.fs.fujitsu.com

As a leading provider of e-business technology solutions, Fujitsu Software Corporation enables its customers to run their companies more competitively with the speed and power of the Internet. Using the company's business process automation technology, enterprise management products, application development tools, and e-business monitoring services, Fujitsu Software Corporation's leadership believes that "the possibilities are infinite."

Fujitsu Software Corporation, based in San Jose, California, has been providing its software expertise and international resources to clients across the globe since 1991. A wholly owned subsidiary of global giant Fujitsu Ltd., which was established in 1935 and is comprised of over 500 companies and affiliates dedicated to world-class information technology solutions, Fujitsu Software Corporation leverages its extensive experience and powerful base to develop innovative, high-performing e-business systems.

The company's technology solutions are divided into key product groups. Its COBOL (Common Business Oriented Language) for Windows and UNIX is a complete COBOL development environment that includes a suite of tools for building fast, targeted business systems. Fujitsu COBOL provides significant new Web and development features, such as the Microsoft.NET framework, which enable programmers

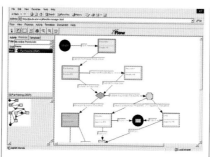

i-Flow™ is a Java-based workflow engine that automates business-to-business and enterprise processes.

and information system developers to take advantage of their existing code for a cutting-edge environment.

Fujitsu Software Corporation's i-Flow™ is a Java-based workflow engine that automates business-to-business (B2B) and enterprise processes. By streamlining, automating, and tracking the practices and procedures of an organization and applying appropriate automation rules, i-Flow enables companies to become more productive, responsive, and profitable. i-Flow utilizes state-of-the-art technologies such

as Java and XML, and is ideal to embed into Web-based applications, helping to deliver key advantages of complete Web-centricity: ease of management, deployment, participation, integration, and adherence to open standards.

The INTERSTAGE™ suite of products provides an enterprise application integration server and framework for integrating distributed applications. The product enables users to collaborate across organizations and networks with customers, partners, and suppliers. INTERSTAGE's capabilities benefit a wide range of businesses, including clients in financial services, manufacturing, distribution, telecommunications, and insurance.

QoEtient™ is a state-of-the-art Web site–management service that delivers Quality of Experience information to e-businesses. The service helps to solve management problems for entrepreneurs, Web site–hosting companies, and Internet service providers by having strategic Web site monitors

analyze performance and availability. QoEtient generates daily reports, alerts, and notifications that are automatically e-mailed to the customer.

Fujitsu Software Corporation's SystemWalker™ is a comprehensive family of products that provides clients with cutting-edge operation-management tools. The highly integrated software is built on policy-based systems management, so customers can establish system-management policies based on their own strategies and goals. SystemWalker covers the entire spectrum of network and systems management.

Tr@nslingo™ is Fujitsu Software Corporation's Web-based Japanese-English translation system that provides fast and accurate translation of Web sites, e-mail messages, and files. When the translation engine is installed on a server on an intranet, the translated results can be accessed from any location over the Internet. Tr@nslingo contains an extensive technical-term dictionary and supports mission-critical documents in a number of areas. For special projects, customers can build and control their own dictionaries.

Like its parent company, Fujitsu Software Corporation is focusing its state-of-the-art products on the possibilities and power of the Internet. By helping its customers successfully handle their business applications on the Internet—in Fujitsu Ltd.'s words, "Everything on the Internet"—they are enabling organizations around the world to streamline their operations, increase productivity, and get valuable products to market faster.

ADAPTEC, INC.

www.adaptec.com

Every day, over the Internet, countless pieces of information stream around the world. Facts. Figures. Questions. Answers. Our information-driven society is becoming increasingly networked—and demanding more and better solutions to move, manage, and protect the information we need.

Small Computer System Interface (SCSI), or "scuzzy," a connection from a PC to a hard drive and other peripherals

Adaptec, Inc., of Milpitas, California, is meeting that demand by bringing innovative storage solutions to a broad, "mainstream" market. The company designs, manufactures, and distributes host bus adapters and controllers that connect servers, workstations, and desktops to storage devices; RAID (Redundant Array of Inexpensive, or Independent, Disks), which boost computer performance and protect data stored on disk drives; and CD recording and data protection

software. Adaptec's products are important parts of the computers made by the leading manufacturers, including Dell, Hewlett-Packard, Gateway, and IBM. They are also critical in high-performance networks, servers, and workstations.

Founded in 1981, Adaptec first realized most of its revenues from producing SCSI, or Small Computer System Interface, chips and boards. This technology allows you to connect various internal and external devices, such as hard disk drives, scanners, and laser printers, to a computer or server, making the transfer of information possible. But recently the company repositioned itself. Now, on its 20th anniversary as a leader in the data storage industry, Adaptec provides end-to-end storage solutions—not just hardware, but software too—to manage and protect data and digital content for e-business and Internet applications.

The company is organized into three business segments: Direct Attached Storage, or DAS; Storage Networking Solutions, or SNS; and Desktop Solutions. The DAS group designs, develops, manufactures, and markets I/O, or input/output, products for servers and workstations. The I/O system connects a computer's central processing unit, or CPU, to both internal and external storage devices. Signals are received and transmitted via adapter cards and controller chips. Adaptec is the leader in high-performance SCSI host bus adapters, and is developing next-generation products that will increase data storage speeds and improve data

integrity even further. In addition, its RAID technology is known for preventing downtime and for providing "data insurance." These benefits are increasingly important with the growing use of the Internet and the growing size of multimedia files. Adaptec's mission is to make RAID accessible, affordable, and easy to install and administer—from entry-level RAID to enterprise-level RAID for the most demanding environments.

The Storage Networking Solutions division focuses on storage solutions beyond the server. Because the demands of the Internet are so huge, no single server platform can meet all data storage requirements. Storage is moving "outside the box," and Adaptec is providing new answers in the form of Fibre Channel, IP Storage, and InfiniBand™ solutions to give customers storage networking choices in performance, price, manageability, and scalability. These emerging technologies and products will enable several "thin" servers to be connected to a network-like fabric and that fabric to external storage, allowing high-performance interoperable and distributed storage. The range of coming solutions will also offer customers choices in lower-cost data management and increased data availability.

Adaptec's Desktop business segment designs and develops storage and connectivity solutions for personal computers and optical peripherals. These include SCSI, USB (universal serial bus), and Firewire (IEEE-1394) products and solutions that enable

external storage connectivity, and RAID solutions for enhanced data performance and protection.

In late 2000, Adaptec spun off its Software business unit to form a separate subsidiary, Roxio. This action has enabled both companies to execute independently focused strategies. Adaptec's software products include Easy CD Creator™, Toast™, and Jam™ for CD recording, and GoBack™, a system-recovery utility for PCs.

President and CEO Robert N. Stephens believes that Adaptec will continue to be "at the forefront of change" as storage becomes an increasingly critical element in people's business and personal lives. Storage will take on a greater ease of use, and currently emerging technologies will make it more reliable and more versatile. New RAID technology, in particular, may enable data storage and protection to become affordable and easy to install and administer by all.

HITACHI, LTD.

www.hds.com
www.hitachi.com
www.hii-hitachi.com
www.hitachi.com/semiconductor

Nearly a hundred years ago, in 1910, one of the largest electronics/electrical equipment companies was founded—far from Silicon Valley. Today, however, Japan's Hitachi, Ltd., is a major presence both in Silicon Valley and throughout the world, providing a broad range of cutting-edge products and services to customers in every corner of the globe. Following the commitment of Hitachi's founders to enrich the future—"Though we cannot live one hundred years, we should be concerned about one thousand years hence"—today's leadership strives to produce advanced products that are built to last, provide superior solutions, and improve the quality of life.

Nearly everywhere you look—homes, hospitals, factories, supermarkets, highways, and city streets—you are likely to find a Hitachi product. Hitachi's more than 330,000 employees in the organization's more than 1,000 companies develop, manufacture, and sell everything from appliances to bullet trains to

The E10A emulator is one of Hitachi's many development tools that facilitate the rapid and efficient transformation of design ideas into robust, high-quality embedded products.

hydraulic turbines to automotive parts to semiconductors. President Etsuhiko Shoyama currently oversees a diverse, state-of-the-art supercompany with revenues approaching $70 billion.

Hitachi, Ltd., first brought its widespread expertise to the United States when it exported 30 electric fans to America in 1924. Thirty-five years later, the company established a New York presence, Hitachi New York, to sell turbines and power generators. Then, in 1969, Hitachi New York became Hitachi America, Ltd., to reflect the division's national scope. Soon, computers and semiconductors became the major focus of Hitachi America's operations. Hitachi America (www.hitachi.com) is currently the largest subsidiary outside Asia and employs some 6,000 people in North America.

Over the next several decades, Hitachi continued to grow and expand its American presence, opening offices and subsidiaries throughout the U.S. Today, Hitachi has a total of close to 16,000 employees in some 70 companies in North America. The company's product lines include leading-edge technology for the automotive, computer, power generation, life sciences, semiconductor, multimedia systems, consumer electronics, and telecommunications industries.

Several of Hitachi, Ltd.'s and Hitachi America's subsidiaries are strategically located in Silicon Valley. Santa Clara–based Hitachi Data Systems Corporation (www.hds.com) markets a wide range of information technology (IT) solutions that are aimed at

The revolutionary Hitachi DZ-MV100A is the world's first tapeless optical disc-based full-motion video and mega-pixel still camera. This digital camcorder can record up to two hours of full-motion MPEG2 video and nearly 2,000 mega-pixel still images. The DVDCAM uses Maxell's 8 cm DVD-RAM disc, which is compatible with the new generation of Hitachi's DVD-ROM (GD-7500). The camera's random access capability enables easy editing and viewing.

providing customers with superior business agility. The company delivers enterprise storage systems and services that enable Global 1000 businesses to stay at the top of their competitive markets.

Because the leaders of Hitachi Data Systems realized that clients needed help to manage the enormous amounts of data that have accompanied the growing use of the Internet, the company reorganized recently to focus on this key area. Now clients have the products they require to maintain continuous access to every piece of their data, to respond more quickly to customer service requests, and to keep their IT infrastructure up and performing. Not only does Hitachi Data Systems deliver the hardware for a solid, reliable IT system but the powerful, comprehensive software to manage it.

Two breakthrough products from Hitachi Data Systems are the Hitachi Freedom Storage™ Lightning 9900™ and the Hitachi Freedom Storage Thunder 9200™. Both provide Hitachi's SAN (storage area network) architecture and support for multiple platforms, including UNIX and Windows NT. They also meet clients' needs for storage

without limits. The Hitachi Freedom Storage Lightning 9900 series, which offers advanced enterprise storage systems with instant, continuous access to data, is based on a unique "internal switch" architecture that enables users to grow storage capacity as high as 37 terabytes in a single system without experiencing any slowdown in performance. The products come with a 100% data availability guarantee, and can be attached—either directly or through a network—to a wide variety of operating system platforms such as Windows 2000 and NT, and many versions of UNIX, Linux, Novell, and OS/390. They provide information delivery from any computer anywhere, any time. A full complement of software supports business continuity, database backup, and application testing.

The Hitachi Freedom Storage Thunder 9200 delivers to mid-size companies the fast, reliable, high-capacity storage that was previously available only to enterprise customers. Clients with growing data storage needs now have the option of a system with high scalability and reduced complexity, and the speedy information delivery they need to get their products to market more quickly.

Another Hitachi America subsidiary, Hitachi Semiconductor (America) Inc. (www.hitachi.com/semiconductor), is also headquartered in Silicon Valley. The San Jose–based company offers a full line of products for the embedded marketplace. With their leadership established by the SuperH® RISC Processor and H8 Microcontroller product families, Hitachi Semiconductor provides superior products to the world's leading electronic-device manufacturers in many industrial, automotive, networking, and consumer markets. Beyond semiconductors, Hitachi can offer a total system solution with SRAMs, Flash memories, Flash and MultiMedia cards, and EEPROMs; logic ICs; discrete devices; MOSFETs; communication ICs; RF/wireless ICs; and mass storage ICs.

Hitachi Semiconductor, together with its sister organizations in Japan, Europe, and Asia, maintains a leading position consistently ranking in the top 10 of the largest semiconductor companies. With extensive global research and development resources and state-of-the-art manufacturing processes, its cutting-edge components are able to meet engineering demands and provide advanced silicon solutions to both today's and tomorrow's applications. As a member of the Hitachi global family, Hitachi Semiconductor (America) helps bring the world's best technology to U.S. customers.

Hitachi Instruments, Inc. (www.hii-hitachi.com), a San Jose–based subsidiary, markets and sells a wide range of

The Hitachi Freedom Storage Thunder 9200 system is designed for mid-size businesses. It is a high-performance, high-reliability system offering users the capacity to store up to 7.1 terabytes of data.

analytical and biomedical instrumentation throughout the United States. The company's personnel continually work to find new solutions to scientific application challenges. Products fall into six different categories: analytical instrumentation, clinical diagnostics, DNA sequencers, diffraction gratings, electron microscopy, and electron-beam lithography.

Systems developed by the Analytical Instrumentation group are used to analyze materials used in the fields of drug discovery, natural products, and food analysis. These systems include liquid chromatography systems, which identify the components of chemical mixtures; purification systems; and amino acid analyzers, which are used in biochemistry, food, medical, and pharmaceutical research. The company's Clinical Instrumentation Products group develops analyzers and accessories that are used in clinical blood analysis. The Diffraction Gratings group provides products that can analyze different kinds of radiation, ranging from x-rays to infrared. Hitachi

diffraction gratings have been used by the Okazaki National Research Institute in a spectrograph that analyzed the world's largest artificial rainbow as well as in a spectrometer that was part of an ultraviolet exploration device launched by NASA.

Since Hitachi developed the first electron microscope in Japan in 1941, the company has produced advanced electron microscopes that continue to receive praise in the scientific and industrial communities. The Electron Microscopy Products group currently develops electron microscopes for electron transmission, scanning, and measurement; the microscopes are used in conjunction with the purification of synthetic products. The Electron-Beam Lithography group develops etching systems used in the mass production of 130–150nm semiconductor devices and systems that use electron and ion beams to measure and evaluate semiconductor wafer particles.

Other Hitachi companies that dot the Silicon Valley landscape include

Hitachi Chemical, Hitachi Metals, Hitachi Software Engineering and Hitachi Electronics Engineering, Hitachi Computer Products (America), Hitachi America Capital, Hitachi Digital Graphics, Kokosai Electric, and MiraiBio Inc.

With its many subsidiaries and divisions, Hitachi, Ltd., and its key American presence, established through Hitachi America and Hitachi Data Systems, have become a driving force behind the richness and extensiveness of electronic and electrical products. While it maintains this premier position, the company also works to create an environment that enables its employees to reach their full potential, and to be involved in innovative programs that improve the quality of life in the communities in which they live. Like the mark designed for the company's founding—one Chinese character that means "sun" and a second character that means "rise"—Hitachi, Ltd., is meeting the challenges of the 21st century by working to create a better future for all.

Hitachi's flagship SuperH RISC Processor, of the SH3-DSP series, in a Quad Flat Package, installed on a Cisco board

AUTODESK

www.autodesk.com

Whether they design bicycles in California, maps for the U.S. Air Force, or new buildings in Singapore, companies around the world rely on Autodesk software for their digital design needs. The company's renowned design tools, including the highly acclaimed AutoCAD®, make a wide range of design projects run more smoothly and efficiently.

Ultrasonic testing of the Angkor Wat temples measures levels of decay and records the data for import into AutoCAD software.

Founded in 1982, Autodesk is now the world's leading design and digital content–creation company. Its products are used by more than 4,000,000 customers, including 94% of the Fortune 500's largest industrial and service corporations. While its core business is desktop design software, the company is now transforming the design process by helping its customers incorporate the benefits of the Internet. "The changes Autodesk is making will significantly enhance our customers' productivity and competitiveness," says chairman and CEO Carol Bartz.

The software produced by the San Rafael, California, company keeps design information flowing. As AmericaOne, the fastest U.S. entry in the America's Cup race was being designed, the AutoCAD platform was the software of choice. The innovative program allowed the boat's specifications to be drafted and the race conditions simulated years before the boat entered the water. The Autodesk® View program allowed the design team—naval architects, fluid engineers, and yacht designers located across the U.S.—to share exact drawings in real time with crew members and building contractors in New Zealand and California via the Internet. Virtually every part of the boat was built after first being designed with Autodesk software.

For many cars as well as boats, Autodesk software is key to the parts design process. Hirotech, Inc., a Japan-based leader in automotive manufacturing, uses Autodesk's Mechanical Desktop™ software to design Mazda car doors. Before using Mechanical Desktop, the company's product cycle time was close to a month—there were long waits for drawings and varying interpretations of the designers' ideas. Now the cycle time

Erosion and damage are tracked using the multiple layer feature of AutoCAD.

is just two weeks, and design data is conveyed in 3-D renderings that show exactly how the product will look and perform. Mechanical Desktop can also show engineers if there will be interference between a unit's various parts.

Autodesk software is also touted for its building restoration capabilities. At Angkor Wat, the 270-temple sandstone treasure built in Cambodia in the twelfth century, restoration work has been ongoing since 1987. Before AutoCAD software was put into use in 1997, handwritten records documented all restoration efforts. Using the software, international team members are now able to visually mimic those records as well as record continuing decay and restoration data. Photos that document the work are scanned at high resolution and stored on CD-ROMs, with each type of decay recorded independently. Then color and hatch patterns are coded into the computer as invisible layers over the photos. When analyzing environmental effects, such as the correlation between water runoff and salt buildup, just the relevant layers can be viewed. The program can also calculate the surface area of a specific building zone to determine how much of a chemical is needed for remediation.

At the Jet Propulsion Laboratory (JPL), in Pasadena, California, design is a critical part of the lab's development of spacecraft. JPL's vehicles have visited every known planet except Pluto, providing scientists with invaluable information for scientific, medical, industrial, and commercial applications. But engineers at JPL are continually being asked to design components that are smaller, more efficient, and more cost effective. To meet those demands, engineers are using Autodesk design tools that enable a wide range of specialists to analyze design problems and assess multiple design scenarios on the spot. The software can also simulate orbits and enable designers to analyze sensor placement with customers. Design quality has improved, and customer savings have increased by a factor of four.

To further improve design and design collaboration, Autodesk is enabling its customers to work with the Internet. The company has Web-aware desktop products, browser-based products, and Internet portals and marketplaces to help its customers integrate the Web. Leveraging digital design data through Internet and desktop design tools to increase productivity and enhance business processes is the key driver for Autodesk customers in the future, to achieve competitive advantage through design.

autodesk®

APPLE

Since its founding in 1976, Cupertino, California–based Apple has been committed to bringing the best possible computing experiences to students, educators, creative professionals, and consumers around the world. This commitment inspired Apple's 1984 introduction of the original Macintosh®,

Steven Wozniak's 1970s workshop. When Mike Markkula visited the Woz and Steve Jobs for the first time, he remembers that he saw "the world's first single-board computer, the whole computer on one board. It was the first computer to have RAM on the main circuit board. It was the first computer that had a programming language built in, in ROM. It was the first computer that interacted seamlessly with an NTSC television set. It was the first computer that had color graphics, or any graphics."

which single-handedly changed the way people interact with computers to work, learn, and play.

Today, Apple continues to build on more than two decades of innovation with revolutionary desktop and portable computers, cutting-edge applications, Internet services, and a refined operating system, the Mac® OS.

In 1998, Apple introduced iMac™, which today is the world's most popular desktop computer for the home and classroom. Available in distinctive colors, iMac offers the fastest, easiest way to the Internet, with a set-up assistant that helps users get online within minutes. iMac features iMovie™ 2, Apple's groundbreaking digital video editing software; high-performance PowerPC G3 processors; a fanless design that reduces noise levels to half that of competitors'; and built-in all-digital speakers. iBook™, the "iMac to go," is the first portable computer built with the needs of students, educators, and consumers in mind. iBook features a unique rugged design, iMovie 2 software, and super-fast PowerPC G3 processors. Available in several bright colors, iBook offers battery life of up to six hours, instant Internet access, and support for Apple's revolutionary AirPort™ wireless networking solution.

Apple's digital video editing software, iMovie 2, lets users import video from a digital video camcorder directly into their FireWire®-enabled iBook or iMac. They can then rearrange clips and add special effects such as cross dissolves and scrolling titles. Completed iMovies can be stored on the computer, transferred

back to a camcorder for viewing on a TV or videotape, or shared with friends and family via Apple's iTools.

iTools is a new category of free Internet services from Apple and available only at www.apple.com. Apple's four iTools are iDisk, which offers 20 megabytes of free Internet-based storage on Apple's Internet Servers; HomePage, a way to build a personal Web site in less than 10 minutes; Mac.com, an e-mail service; and KidSafe, a breakthrough way to protect kids from unsuitable material on the Internet.

Mac users can choose to access the Internet via AirPort, Apple's cutting-edge wireless networking system. Apple's AirPort solution includes the AirPort Card, which fits inside all Apple computers; and the AirPort Base Station, which contains a 56K modem and an Ethernet port for connecting to a phone line, cable modem, DSL modem, or local-area network. As many as 10 Macs can share a single AirPort Base Station simultaneously from up to 150 feet away, eliminating the need for cables, additional phone lines, or complicated hardware.

In addition to its state-of-the-art consumer hardware and software products, Apple also offers high-end computers for professionals and "pro-sumers." An entirely new class of computer, Apple's Power Mac G4 Cube delivers the supercomputer performance of a Power Mac G4—the first mainstream computer to ship standard with dual processors—in an 8-inch cube. The G4 Cube features the powerful PowerPC G4 processor with Velocity Engine™ that

reaches supercomputer speeds of over 3 billion calculations per second. Suspended in an innovative crystal-clear enclosure that is less than one-fourth the size of most PCs, the G4 Cube's entire electronics assembly can be easily lifted out within seconds, providing access to every major component and enabling easy addition of the AirPort Card. Like iMac, the G4 Cube features a revolutionary cooling design that allows it to run in virtual silence.

What CEO Steve Jobs describes as "the future of the Macintosh" is Mac OS X, the next-generation operating system for the Mac. Mac OS X features Apple's new user interface Aqua™, which combines superior ease of use with great new functionality, including the Dock, which organizes applications, documents, and miniaturized windows. Incorporating state-of-the-art technology, Mac OS X provides memory protection, multitasking, a powerful new graphics engine, and a new version of QuickTime™ software for streaming audio and video. The Mac OS X continues Apple's tradition of developing creative, breakthrough products that put the power of the computer—easily—into the hands of the people using it.

SOUND ADVANTAGE LLC

www.soundadvantage.com

Every office relies upon a variety of technology—phone systems, fax machines, voice mail, e-mail, and contact relationship management software—to maintain the all-important lines of communication with customers, suppliers, and employees. Unfortunately, these systems run independently of each other, are often difficult to operate, and, in most instances, cannot be accessed from outside the office.

Michael Metcalf, the founder of Irvine, California–based Sound Advantage, observed that office technology had not lived up to its promise to free us from our desks and to allow us to be more productive. He witnessed that callers to his business were frustrated with not being able to reach a "live" person and were tired of playing "phone tag." He saw that his own employees were handcuffed by their inability to quickly and efficiently access their voice mail, e-mail, and fax messages, and watched as they struggled to make use of all but the simplest features of the expensive hardware and software purchased to support them.

So, in 1997, Metcalf formed Sound Advantage, and worked for more than two years with his team researching and developing a voice-activated product that would unify disparate communication systems and allow office technology to deliver on its original promise. In 1999, Sound Advantage released SANDi™—the Sound Advantage

SANDi™ (Sound Advantage Natural Dialog Interface) unlocks the power of technology by voice-activating all office communications.

Natural Dialog Interface.

SANDi is a voice-user interface that gives users the power to speak to their technology. SANDi integrates a telephone system with an organization's contact management database, e-mail, fax, PBX, and voice mail.

Responding to simple verbal instructions, the core version of SANDi answers, screens, and routes incoming calls; takes messages; locates employees not at their desks; and dials telephone numbers. SANDi also allows employees to pick up e-mail, voice mail, and fax messages from any phone or computer; forward, save, or delete messages; and call internal and external contacts, all through simple spoken commands.

The original SANDi system was designed for use by small and mid-size offices, but current SANDi products can handle the communication needs of enterprises with several thousand users. Network SANDi expands voice-activated, unified messaging to telephone companies, Internet service providers, and wireless service providers.

Since its launch in 1999, SANDi has won more than 20 industry awards and has garnered much praise from the computer telephony industry. *Computer Telephony* magazine named SANDi

a Product of the Year in both 1999 and 2000. *Teleconnect* magazine named SANDi a Product of the Year for 2000 and awarded SANDi a Computer Telephony Expo 2000 Best of Show designation. SANDi has also won the CTI Product of the Year award and TMC Labs' Innovation Award for 2000.

SANDi was developed to make business communication simple, efficient, and user friendly, but it has quickly shown that it can also enhance the many benefits of technology. By eliminating barriers between different communication systems, SANDi increases productivity, saves time, and gives any office or network a competitive edge. SANDi is a Unified Office Solution™ that handles the communication needs of today's diverse, on-the-go work force with a winning combination of cutting-edge technology and the friendliness of the human voice.

Michael D. Metcalf, founder, president, and CEO of Sound Advantage

TREND MICRO, INC.

www.antivirus.com

While technological advances have made it possible for people around the world to send e-mail, shares files and databases, and download information from many sources, they've also unleashed a worldwide problem—new ways of spreading damaging computer viruses. Such viruses, including the recent and devastating "I Love You" and "Melissa" viruses, have the potential to cause billions of dollars in lost data and productivity and create havoc in the electronic world.

In 1988, Steve Chang, chairman and chief executive officer of Trend Micro, Inc., founded the company with the mission of developing antivirus software for personal computers. As the Internet and corporate networks moved to center stage, Chang redirected Trend Micro's focus toward addressing total network security. This included antivirus and Internet content security solutions for Internet gateways, e-mail, and file servers, and for desktop computers. Today Chang's company continues to develop products that provide integrated antivirus security at all access points of a network, and is working to design security into the infrastructure of the Internet.

Early viruses were pieces of executable code that were spread via the "sneakernet"—users passing them along on floppy diskettes. With the advent of the World Wide Web and e-mail, virus distribution suddenly became even easier—it could be done quickly, and with no geographical bounds.

Viruses grew more and more sophisticated through the use of programming shortcuts such as macros and JavaScript applets for e-mail, documents, and Web pages. Viruses also became able to manipulate e-mail programs, mailing themselves to other users or delivering stolen information to their creators. By the year 2000, the antivirus research community detected an estimated 500 new malicious programs every month. It is expected that viruses and other malicious code will continue to plague computer users through the Internet and Internet-based e-mail.

Unlike products that detect viruses at the desktop, Trend Micro's products block and delete viruses before the desktop is reached. The company's InterScan® product family sits at the Internet gateway server checking all Web traffic, e-mail, and downloads. ScanMail® examines all e-mail traveling in and out of the mail server, supporting such popular messaging systems as Microsoft Exchange and Lotus Notes. OfficeScan™ and PC-cillin® incorporate the same protection for corporate desktop and home users.

Stopping viruses before they enter an organization's systems protects everyone in the organization as well as prevents them from becoming unwitting distributors. Central management capabilities allow automatic software updates from Trend Micro's Web site and rapid deployment to all network users, reducing the time and effort needed to maintain virus protection. TrendLabs, Trend Micro's antivirus research and support center comprised of virus-research teams working 24/7 on three continents, ensures a quick response to new virus threats.

Because e-mail has become such a prevalent form of communication among coworkers, there is growing concern that sexually or racially offensive material may be distributed within organizations, and that "eyes only" documents may go beyond their intended audience. Trend Micro also focuses on content-filtering technologies to provide users with an overall safe Internet experience. The company's eManager™ content-filtering module can block messages and attachments containing inappropriate language or content. eManager can also be used to stop "spam" (electronic junk mail) and block infected e-mails during a virus outbreak until detection is available. WebManager® and AppletTrap™ regulate access to unproductive or illicit Web sites and prevent downloads of malicious Java code hidden within Web pages.

Having revolutionized protection awareness from the desktop to the server, Trend Micro continues in its efforts to build a secure infrastructure for the Internet. The eDoctor™ Global Network initiative aligns leading technology service providers with Trend Micro's products, bringing round-the-clock virus protection and content security to millions of Internet users through such business partners as Qwest and Oracle. The company is also recognized for lending its expertise to the antivirus research community and government councils on cyber-safety. In addition it is currently developing security solutions for emerging technologies, such as wireless and broadband Internet access, to secure future computing environments.

From its headquarters in Tokyo and its major business offices in Cupertino, California, and other locations in North and South America, Europe, Asia, and Australia, Trend Micro is striving to contribute to the overall health of the Internet, working to reduce the likelihood of computer virus infection for both businesses and consumers.

Trend Micro, Inc.'s North American headquarters are located in Cupertino, California.

NETWORK APPLIANCE

www.netapp.com

Before 1992, the computer term "network appliance" had not yet been invented. But during that year, a company called Network Appliance was established. The company was the vision of cofounders Dave Hitz and James Lau, and was based on an exciting idea: to simplify the way data is stored on computers.

The concept was simple but revolutionary. Its development was also timely because of the explosion of the Internet and the huge amounts of information that needed to be stored and delivered on networks. Network Appliance began producing products that quickly and cost-effectively managed and distributed information, and is now the leading supplier of network storage and content delivery solutions. The company's products are designed to scale and simplify the data-management needs of Fortune 500 companies.

Network Appliance's technology has been called "disruptive" because it changes the way companies do business. Instead of using general-purpose computers, many corporations now realize that there are great benefits to using single-purpose computing devices and appliances, known as filers. Network Appliance filers work with a file rather than with a physical data block, which means they can store data from any server, application, or operating system. And because of their small size and lower price, rooms full of slow, costly equipment are no longer needed to keep an organization's data flowing quickly and reliably.

The company has established a strong worldwide presence in just eight years. Headquartered in Sunnyvale, California, Network Appliance's distribution channels span more than 60 countries, and its 2,000 employees are located in major cities around the globe. More than 15,500 Network Appliance™ systems have been installed in such diverse organizations as Yahoo!, Lockheed-Martin, Bear Stearns, and Motorola. *Fortune Magazine* recognized Network Appliance as the fourth fastest-growing company on its list of 100 Fastest Growing Companies for two years in a row, and included Network Appliance in its list of the top 50 e-businesses to watch.

Network Appliance systems enable businesses to simplify, share, and scale their storage networking and content delivery infrastructure without limits. The company does this by providing filers, solutions that improve the storage and accessibility of data on a network; and content delivery appliances, which move data closer to users, improving Internet performance. All of the company's products are designed for multiplatform computing environments, and can handle data from Windows NT® systems, UNIX® systems, and the World Wide Web.

The systems Network Appliance provides let their customers move data easily from filers in a primary data center to filers in a secondary data center, and to content delivery appliances in remote offices. The content delivery appliances

Network Appliance's world headquarters located in Sunnyvale, California

manage, store, and deliver terabytes (trillions of bytes) of content for the users of the customer's network.

Network Appliance's products and services are in demand for several reasons. One is that networking data is becoming ever more diverse, with a huge increase in the available number of applications and data types. Because people can access that data from numerous devices, including cell phones, wireless PDAs, and the Internet, systems are needed that can manage and distribute large amounts of disparate data quickly and accurately.

A second reason is that many companies now have branch offices and operations not only throughout the United States but in Europe, the Middle East, Asia, and many other parts of the world. Employees in these geographically dispersed areas want and need to communicate with each other, so systems must be in place that will push data to them, as well as business partners and other professionals who require it.

Network Appliance's filers serve up data at an availability rate of more than 99.99%. This availability saves corporate networks from costly downtime and allows users to accomplish tasks more quickly. The filers are designed for easy manageability, and to scale to handle from 50 GB to multiple terabytes of data. The entry-level enterprise filer delivers power to departmental applications, such as software development, computer-aided design (CAD), and simulation applications. The mid-range enterprise filer is designed for small- to medium-sized companies, and can support up to 3 TB (terabytes) of data. The large-scale enterprise filer can support the most demanding applications, up to 12 TB of data, and enables enterprise-wide data consolidation. The large-scale clustered enterprise filer provides top performance to multiple networks.

All of Network Appliance's filers provide integrated RAID (redundant array of independent disks), which protects against disk failures and disruption of service. They also feature Snapshot™ technology, which enables near-instantaneous, transparent online backup. Snapshot also lets users quickly recover deleted or modified files, and requires very little disk space. The company's SnapRestore™ software makes it possible to recover terabytes of data in minutes rather than hours. And its SnapMirror™ software provides remote mirroring, or copying to remote locations, at high speeds over local-area or wide-area networks.

Network Appliance's NetCache™ content delivery products enable today's advanced networks to provide high-speed content delivery. They help to solve the largest company's most complex data delivery problems, spanning an entire network, from central headquarters to the most remotely located office. NetCache appliances speed along both audio and video streams, enabling such applications as online training, executive broadcasts, and video on demand. The wide range of features they offer makes it possible for organizations, no matter their size or focus, to custom tailor their system. NetCache products reduce redundant traffic and free up Web and streaming servers, which cuts down greatly on traffic bottlenecks and improves service. NetCache technology also prevents common network attacks, and provides activity filtering and logging.

Another of Network Appliance's data storage delivery solutions is its Data ONTAP™ software. This operating system ensures data availability while reducing the complexity of managing data storage. The software's technology makes certain that network transactions are not lost, and provides fast response times to user requests. Network Appliance filers running Data ONTAP software

Network Appliance employee stands watch in the company's state-of-the-art server room.

easily integrate with existing systems and maximize access to data, as well as allow customers to grow their storage capacity as needed. Data ONTAP has the Write Anywhere File Layout (WAFL™) file system built in. This system allows the addition of storage into the filer while the environment is live, avoiding user downtime.

While some companies improve only parts of their information management systems as their business grows, Network Appliance management believes that an efficient, cost-effective "end-to-end" data infrastructure is the best way to manage and deliver information. Its systems can expand to handle large quantities of data without adding additional administrators, which lowers the cost of system ownership. And because Network Appliance filers and content delivery products are not dependent on any particular operating system, they can meet the needs of most any computing architecture. They are also designed to manage information across a wide range of appliances seamlessly.

In an age of increasing amounts of data, increasing network bottlenecks, and increasing network user dissatisfaction, Network Appliance is providing its customers with a new level of network intelligence through intelligent data management and delivery. CEO Dan Warmenhoven believes that next-generation enterprises understand that the enterprise infrastructure is now the network, and that no one understands how to store and manage content on that network better than Network Appliance.

SONICblue INCORPORATED

www.sonicblue.com

While the business world often reaps the benefits of the breathtaking advances being made in technology, new high-tech products aren't for the corporate environment alone. Devices such as personal organizers, digital audio players, and home networking products help consumers everywhere pursue interests and enjoy their leisure time.

The Nike psa/play 120 is the first digital audio player designed for the athlete.

SONICblue, a Santa Clara, California–based business, is focused on revolutionizing consumer technology. In 1989, the company was founded as S3, and pioneered the field of graphics chip technology. But 10 years later, after becoming the world's largest chip company, S3 began to realign itself around the Internet. CEO and chairman Ken Potashner saw that the pervasive use of the Internet and the increased bandwidth available to the home would enable new types of consumer "information appliances." S3 acquired Diamond Multimedia and established an extensive network of manufacturers and retailers, including Dell, Apple, Circuit City, CompUSA, and Virgin Megastores. Renamed SONICblue in 2000, the company now develops digital media devices, information appliances, home networking products, and Internet access products for the "digitally connected" home.

SONICblue is organized into several business units. One of the company's key business units is based on the Rio® family of handheld digital audio players, the first device of this type in the industry. The newest offerings in the Rio line are the Rio 600 and the Rio 800, both of which provide consumers with an innovative design, numerous music formats, and content from major music partners. From its top market share position, the Rio family is expanding beyond handheld devices with the Rio Receiver and new digital audio devices for automotive markets.

SONICblue's Access business unit delivers high-speed, innovative connectivity and home networking products. The Diamond™ Mako is a Web-connected personal digital assistant (PDA) that provides e-mail connectivity and Web browsing using a travel modem or a phone with an infrared port. The Diamond Mako incorporates an agenda application that features day, week, two-week, and to-do screens as well as a today screen that provides a daily snapshot of important appointments and tasks.

Also produced by the Access unit is the HomeFree™ family of networking products. HomeFree devices enable

With the ability to play over 20 hours of digital audio from one CD, RioVolt™ SP100 allows users to play both standard audio CDs as well as MP3 and WMA files.

consumers to network multiple PCs throughout their home via phone lines to share Internet access. The networked computers can also share content and peripheral devices, and family members can interact in such activities as playing computer games. The HomeFree line of "residential gateways" will provide customers with a one-stop-shopping DSL solution.

Supra is another product family developed by SONICblue's Access business unit. Sold under the Diamond brand, these award-winning dial-up fax/modems support 56K data transmission and are PC and Mac compatible. Both the external and internal products provide fast, reliable Internet connections.

frontpath™, another SONICblue business unit, enables the company to pursue opportunities in the information appliance home and vertical markets. frontpath's forthcoming information appliance, ProGear™, is a portable, wireless, broadband-based product that delivers customized multimedia content. ProGear has a 10.4-inch LCD touchscreen and a handwriting recognition feature, and can act as a personal organizer, download e-books, and connect users with favorite Internet sites.

SONICblue also develops and markets professional graphics accelerators through its Professional Graphics business unit. The company's FireGL™ accelerators are based on IBM's graphics technology and enable enhanced 2-D and 3-D graphics processing for Windows NT and Linux workstations.

SONICblue fosters an entrepreneurial spirit among its Silicon Valley employees. The company aggressively works toward developing new products for consumers who are ready to explore innovative ways to enjoy digital media. SONICblue combines its broad technology capabilities, brands, and financial resources to bring forward leadership products in the converging Internet, digital media, and consumer device markets.

Capture, mix, and play back up to four hours of digital-quality music from the Internet or CDs on the rechargeable Rio 800.

Technological Synergy

In the late Philip Wylie's 1972 novel, *The End of the Dream*, the environmental stresses on the planet ultimately devastated the world as it had been. The author's story line was prophetic: the causes of environmental demise were already at work in the 1970s.

Now, at the turn of the third millennium, the scientific community is in agreement that global warming is occurring rapidly. Many other ecological calamities are also in progress. But the debate over solutions to our environmental woes is mired in economic interests and politics. It is very probable that no effective environmental measures will be enacted without a cataclysmic event.

If we harbor any hope that our children and their children will live on a planet that is healthy, self-renewing, and similar to the planet of our ancestors, that hope is most likely based on research to develop a new technology that will replace the fossil fuels that are slowly warming the earth. But Wylie wrote in his novel of the lack of synergy—interaction between elements that produces an effect that is greater than the sum of the parts—between scientific technologies as a cause of ecological demise. His premise was that an expert in biology has only rudimentary knowledge of nuclear fission or chemistry, and that a Nobel Laureate in chemistry has only an elementary knowledge of physiology. Wylie wrote that if parallel sciences advance without synchronicity, each can act against the other with unforeseen effects. A primary real-world example of such an effect is the melting of Antarctica's ice caps as a result of the use of energy-efficient petroleum products. The scientists who developed these products did not realize that widespread petroleum use would deplete the ozone layer.

Linus Pauling, the world-renowned scientist and Nobel Prize winner, realized the need for synergy and understanding among the various scientific venues. Said Pauling:

> My Ph.D. was in chemistry and mathematical physics, so I had a good basic background . . . [including] nuclear physics, mathematics and chemistry, mineralogy, x-ray crystallography, biology, then later molecular biology, and molecular medicine. Many of the contributions to knowledge that I have made have resulted from my taking information that I have in one field and combining it with information that I have in another field.

Pauling, twice a Nobel Laureate, in chemistry and peace, was the focus of the first in-depth interview conducted by the Santa Clara Valley Historical Association. Because of his wide-ranging expertise and accomplishments, Pauling has been called the 20th century's first "Renaissance man." He reinvented chemistry in the 1920s with his application of quantum physics to the study of chemistry. With his new theory of wave mechanics, he succeeded in explaining molecular science for the first time. Pauling's "resonance theory" proposed that some molecules resonate between different structures, rather than holding to a single fixed structure. This insight made possible the creation of many of the drugs, dyes, plastics, and synthetic fibers that we now take for granted. For his discoveries in chemistry, Linus Pauling was awarded the Nobel Prize in 1954.

After hydrogen bombs were dropped on Hiroshima and Nagasaki in 1945, Pauling studied the effects of radiation. He became convinced that a nuclear war, or even the continued atmospheric testing of nuclear weapons, could do irreparable damage to the environment and the population. Under a veil of government secrecy, the dangers of nuclear testing were concealed from the public. When Pauling spoke out about the harmful effects of radiation, many Americans considered him traitorous. However, the Nobel Laureate continued to educate the public about the hazards of radiation and campaigned for peace, disarmament, and an end to nuclear testing. His efforts cost him many friends, funding for research, and his job of 33 years at Cal Tech.

But in 1962, Linus Pauling was awarded his second Nobel Prize—for peace. Directly because of his efforts, the first Nuclear Test Ban Treaty was enacted. Pauling then continued his work for the good of people everywhere with discoveries relating to vitamins and nutrients. His last great scientific work, up until his death in 1994, involved the positive effect of particular nutrients on heart disease.

Like Linus Pauling, many leaders in Silicon Valley understand that through technology synergy we may find solutions to issues that affect society, including environmental problems. Many Silicon Valley companies make certain that their board of directors seats representatives from various fields, often as diverse as biotechnology, semiconductors, venture capital, and photonics. As time goes forward, some of these companies may find the synergy and the technology necessary to reverse our current environmental fortunes.

Linus Pauling was optimistic: "I believe that we are intelligent enough to be able to solve these problems before they reach the stage of being catastrophic problems . . . I'm optimistic about the future."

"The key event was trying to actually join two different kinds of DNA molecules from totally different organisms in the test tube, something which doesn't happen in nature as far as we know but which can be done now at will. And so today we can construct any combination of genes from any organisms at will. Moreover, we can isolate the genes from any organism on our planet without too much difficulty, and that has given rise to the whole concept and field of biotechnology."

—Paul Berg, Nobel Laureate,
DNA Research

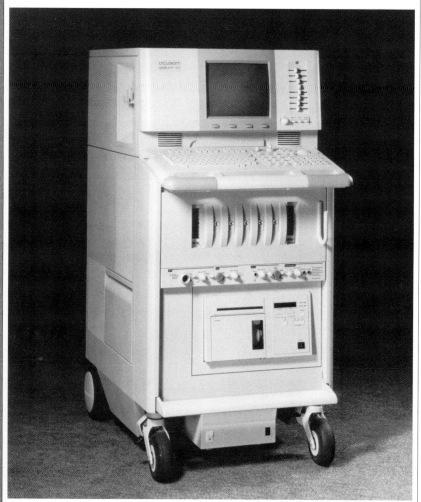

The Acuson® 128XP/10sp diagnostic ultrasound system

THE PROMISE OF TECHNOLOGY IN MEDICINE

While the last years of the 20th century saw significant advances in nearly every aspect of computer technology, the early years of the new millennium are ushering in some of the most spectacular yet. Many of these can be found in the fields of medicine and health care, and are rapidly increasing our ability to live not only well but long. In addition to putting the powers of the integrated circuit to work to improve and enrich our educations, our businesses, and our leisure time, today Silicon Valley technology is also helping to make it more likely that we're going to be around and able to enjoy them.

From diagnostics to surgery, from orthopedics to neurology to oncology and cosmetics, recent achievements in medical technology are improving and saving lives around the globe. Scientists, engineers, researchers, and medical professionals are all contributing to the advancement of the state of the art. Just as computer technology developed dramatically in the 1970s through university, research, and industry leaders sharing knowledge, so too is the field of medical technology advancing through the synergy of many organizations and many minds. Faster computers are leading to advancements in drug research. Developments in laser technology are leading to ever better medical equipment. A discovery in the world of chemistry is leading to the manufacture of a new and more powerful class of drugs.

Through competition, mentoring, research, and "town-gown" ties, much of the world has reaped the rewards of the extraordinary intellect, diversity, and expertise of those who live and work in Silicon Valley. With the explosion of the Internet, those rewards are now reaching even further and coming faster. Particularly in the medical field, the Internet and networking have opened up numerous and important opportunities for advancement. Now colleagues in every part of the world can confer and collaborate, sharing models, working together in real time, extending and improving research studies, teaching, communicating, gaining a global perspective. Patients, too, benefit enormously from Internet access and medical networks. They can research nearly any medical topic, learn about current health-related thinking, become a more informed patient, and have access to physicians or health care providers no matter how far from them they may be. Sophisticated software is contributing enormously to myriad medical and health care strides, from collecting and distributing key data to quality assurance to designing treatment to aiding surgeons during critical procedures. The

In 1998, I was working at Starbucks in the Midwest. I quit my job there, drove out to Silicon Valley, and landed a new job within two weeks that paid five times as much.

Russell Kostner, Software Developer

In 1957, two-year old Gordon Issacs was the first person to be successfully treated by a linear-electronic accelerator for retinoblastona, a form of eye cancer.

Computers made it possible to totally change the way cancer was treated, and today, as a result of digital technology, we're again going through a revolution in cancer treatment. We've developed a technology called intensity-modulated radiation therapy, which makes it possible to sculpt a radiation beam to the exact shape of a tumor within the three-dimensional space in the body and to avoid hitting, as much as possible, any healthy tissue that might be damaged by radiation. This is actually the second revolution in cancer treatment. The first was 30 years ago, when linear accelerators came into being.

Dick Levy, CEO of Varian Medical Systems

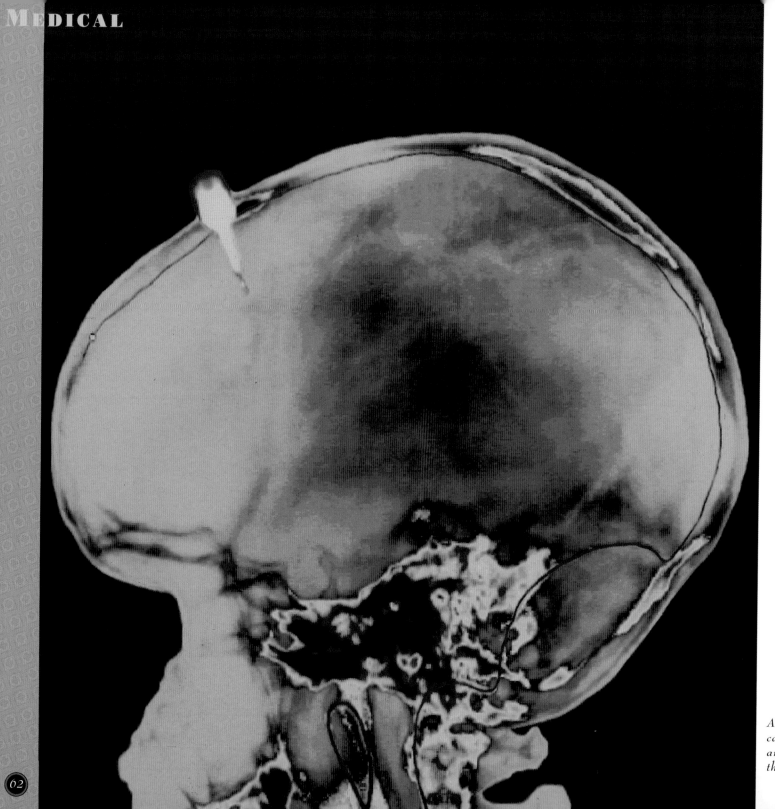

A Target Tracker® catheter winds its way around the perimeter of the patient's brain.

Internet even enables new parents to show off their babies to family and friends across the globe directly from the hospital, soon after the big event.

Two key areas that are currently benefiting greatly from the latest Silicon Valley medical technology are those involving the treatment of cancer and heart disease. Digital technology has produced a revolution in cancer treatment, enabling radiation therapy to be beamed exactly to a tumor site, lessening the damage caused to nearby healthy tissue. Lasers, which produce a coherent beam of light by exciting atoms and causing them to radiate their energy, were first conceived of by Gordon Gould, a graduate student at Columbia University in 1957. The concept behind the laser, however, was studied much earlier by Albert Einstein, in 1916, and by Charles Townes, who built the first device that amplified microwaves by the stimulated emission of radiation.

The first effective laser was built by Theodore Maiman in 1960, and medical uses for the device were discovered soon after. The first medical use was in treating conditions of the eye—reducing the chances of going blind from diabetic retinopathy from 50% to 1%—but now lasers are used to destroy tumors throughout the body, increasing life spans and improving quality of life. Additional technology-based treatments currently under development that are potentially even more beneficial involve implanting radioactive material directly in a tumor site, injecting chemicals into a patient and then hitting the tumor site with laser beams that cause the chemicals to kill the cancer, and using radiation in conjunction with DNA segments.

Greatly advancing the treatment of heart disease are two medical techniques, ultrasound imaging and catheters. Ultrasound imaging, like the laser, was developed in the 1950s and first employed for medical purposes in the 1960s. Using high-frequency sound waves, ultrasound devices can produce images of internal organs and soft tissues, and are particularly well suited for diagnosing heart disease.

Now ultrasound is being used to treat heart disease in conjunction with the catheter, a flexible tube that is inserted into the body. But the catheter's use in the examination of the heart isn't new. In 1904, a German, an American, and a French-American won a Nobel Prize for the use of the catheter in their study of the interior of the heart and the circulatory system. Following in their

Today's computer imagery can display the human body's structural components.

In IVF clinics today, where people go to try to produce an embryo that they can carry to term and have a baby, they collect a man's sperm, a woman's eggs, mix them in a petri plate, the sperm enters the egg, fertilizes it, and you get these little embryos, these little what are called 'blastocysts.' They make a lot of them. But they don't implant all of them, because they don't want to have a woman having eight babies. So they may implant three, and one takes. Sometimes two take. Sometimes they implant five, and three take. So you begin to see these multiple births. But the rest of [the blastocysts] they freeze away in liquid nitrogen, and they sit there for years and years and years. And at some point in these IVF clinics, they've used up all the storage space they have. They go back to the donors and they say, 'Do you want us to implant these?' 'No, we don't want them anymore.' 'Can we destroy them?' 'Yes, you can destroy them.' You sign a paper, informed consent to destroy.

Now, the question that comes up is, those are perfectly useable to generate stem cells. So it is very difficult to understand the ethical or moral outcry that goes with saying, 'No, no, you cannot kill these embryos,' even though they are going to be flushed down the drain—but you can't use them in order to make something that might be very beneficial, which is really very hard to rationalize.

In any case, this is an issue that, in this country, is just still caught up in abortion and the inability to work with human embryos.

Paul Berg,
Nobel Laureate (DNA Research)

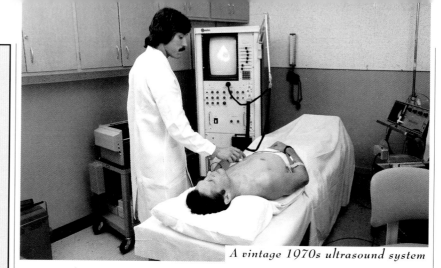

A vintage 1970s ultrasound system

footsteps, other teams and individuals developed and put to use exciting new catheters, the latest of which enables the study of the heart from within. Using reflected ultrasonic waves and a state-of-the-art high-tech system, one type of catheter is now delivering on its promise by allowing physicians to examine the functioning of the heart and to make critical diagnoses of heart disease and irregular heart rhythms. Patient treatment is then aided and managed by the storage of the information in digital format and its outputting to a medical network. People are also benefiting enormously from the newest portable heart defibrillators that enable non-medical personnel to provide life-saving treatment far from hospitals and health care centers.

In a blending of biology and technology, a University of California San Diego research team has used silicon wafers to bring hope to those who suffer from still other serious diseases—those that relate to the liver, including hepatitis C and cancer. The researchers have developed a process that enables liver cells to thrive on specially machined silicon chips, a breakthrough that could lead to the creation of an artificial liver device that could keep patients alive while they wait for a donor organ or even allow their own liver to regenerate naturally. Through research and ingenuity, the same silicon blanks that are used to make semiconductor chips can now be used to provide nutrients and chemicals to as many as 300,000 liver cells on a 0.16-square-inch area.

While history tells us that Egyptian priests before 2000 B.C. developed and codified the world's first sophisticated medical practice, it is the medical innovators of the 21st century, many of whom are in Silicon Valley, who are bringing hope and help to the world community. The potential for continuing technological, medical, and biotechnological discovery is great, and the process of research, testing, design, and manufacture is both flourishing and full of promise.

A test technician trades ideas with Dr. Malcolm A. Bagshaw, professor and chairman of the Department of Radiation Oncology, Stanford University School of Medicine.

From Ancient to Modern Times: Technology as a Catapult for Change

Imagine living in a medieval European village before the waterwheel existed. The men and women of your village work 12 hours a day, six days a week. Good years produce enough wheat to feed everyone. All the wheat is ground into flour by hand, a process that takes hundreds of hours of hard work. When there is a surplus, this flour is either stored or sold to one of the merchants who trade along the nearby river.

Then, one year, the people who live in a village across the river construct a waterwheel. You and the others in your village watch this strange technology turning and working all day and all night. But the villagers across the river don't share the secrets of their new contraption, and you and your family keep harvesting your wheat and grinding it into flour the same way that your forefathers did for generations.

But sometimes the harvest is too small to feed everyone in your village. The outlook is always ominous when this happens. A lack of food brings disease and death.

Within less than two generations, the village that possesses the waterwheel doubles in size. The villagers there produce more grain per acre than those in your village do. They grind finer flour in their gristmill, powered by the waterwheel. River merchants pay them more for their flour. The waterwheel also powers the cutting of timber and a fine-looking town emerges. Your village is still very primitive.

The technology of the waterwheel, which was Syrian in origin and reached medieval Europe from the Islamic Iberian Peninsula, spread slowly at first. But soon the villages that were located next to a river and relied on the power of a waterwheel were the ones that prospered. The waterwheel's effect on population, efficiency, and health was profound. The waterwheel and its improvements set the stage for one of the greatest cultural advancements known in history: the Renaissance.

For as far back as we know, advancements in technology have always propelled a great age. For example, the ability to craft iron in large batches enabled Charlemagne's armies to reunite Europe:

> Writing in the late ninth century, the Monk of St. Gall tells us how in 773 Charlemagne and his host mounted an assault against Pavia, the capital of the Lombard realm. Coming out upon his walls to view the enemy, King Desiderius was overwhelmed by the spectacle of the massed and glittering Frankish weapons: 'Oh, the iron! Alas, the iron!' he cried, and the captain with him fell fainting. While the Monk of St. Gall is notoriously a novelist rather than a historian, nevertheless this episode symbolizes, even if it does not record, Europe's effective transition, under Charlemagne, to the iron age.

Lynn White, Jr., in *Medieval Technology and Social Change*

Following the arrival of Charlemagne's famous iron swords, iron tools became common. Such tools, including the felling ax and the heavy plow, began to be used in medieval agriculture far in excess of tools used in previous civilizations. Every village soon had an ironsmith.

Under Genghis Khan, the Mongols invented and refined a stirrup that allowed a rider to shoot an arrow in any direction while riding his horse. This stirrup produced a great advantage in warfare because the method of attack it enabled was devastating to mounted armored knights and foot soldiers. With great effect, Mongol horsemen could now gallop within range of their enemy, let loose several volleys of arrows, then turn quickly and ride back to safety. The use of this new technology enabled the Mongols to conquer most of Asia.

In the 1400s, Portugal's Prince Henry the Navigator was an important catalyst of new naval technology and exploration. In 1416, he established a school at Sagres, Portugal, at the far southwest corner of Europe. For over 2,000 years, this was a place that seafarers had considered the "end of the world." Beyond this point it was commonly believed that the seas boiled and great monsters swallowed ships and crew. Prince Henry sought out the best astronomers, navigators, seamen, geographers, and scientists of the time. His school became a guarded, tightly controlled research center. His goal was to invent a ship that could sail in the open ocean without capsizing.

At Sagres, Prince Henry and his collaborators constructed the caravel, a vessel capable of sailing the open sea. On board caravels, Prince Henry's captains explored the West African coast, sailed around Cape Verde in 1445, and ventured as far as present-day Sierra Leone, establishing a profitable trade in gold and slaves. Advanced sailing techniques and an increased knowledge of trade winds prepared the way for Portugal's sea power and later explorations to the Americas. The famous maritime explorers Vasco da Gama, Ferdinand Magellan, and Christopher Columbus were all connected to the school at Sagres, Portugal.

VARIAN MEDICAL SYSTEMS

www.varian.com

The name Varian and the word "pioneer" have been tightly linked for more than 50 years. In 1948, Varian Associates, Inc., was founded by Russell and Sigurd Varian and other Stanford University researchers who pioneered the development of commercial applications for two technologies that were emerging at the time: the klystron tube, which became the foundation for radar and microwave communication; and nuclear magnetic resonance (NMR), which has led to great advancements in molecular research. The company then went on to pioneer the use of medical linear accelerators—devices that use electromagnetic waves to speed up electrons in a specially designed tube to hit a target and generate x-rays—for cancer treatment. Next came innovative work developing analytical instruments, vacuum products, and semiconductor manufacturing products. And today, after spinning off its instrument and semiconductor businesses in 1999, the renamed Varian Medical Systems company is pioneering yet another great advancement—Intensity Modulated Radiation Therapy, or IMRT.

Varian calls its therapy SmartBeam™ IMRT, technology that has moved from the experimental stage to the clinical stage in only the last few years. While it is not yet used extensively—currently IMRT is employed in about two dozen leading-edge hospitals throughout the United

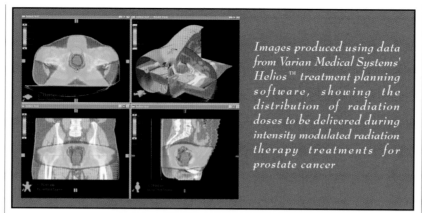

Images produced using data from Varian Medical Systems' Helios™ treatment planning software, showing the distribution of radiation doses to be delivered during intensity modulated radiation therapy treatments for prostate cancer

States—the powerful new technology not only produces fewer side effects, but shows promise for greatly improving cancer cure rates. Experts tout the technology as able to destroy many types of tumors while minimizing the damage done to healthy tissue nearby, and believe it will change the field of radiation cancer treatment. In fact, for certain types of tumors, radiotherapy may soon begin to replace surgery as the preferred form of treatment.

Radiation has been used to treat cancer for over a hundred years, when it was discovered that radioactivity and x-rays could damage cancerous cells by interfering with their ability to grow and reproduce. However, until digital diagnostic imaging, powerful computers, and specialized software were available, it was impossible to focus radiation beams only on the cancerous tumor and minimize damage to surrounding healthy tissue.

With the advent of IMRT, clinicians can now precisely target tumor cells, spare non-cancerous tissues, and deliver higher doses of radiation that improve the chances of completely eradicating tumors. Using IMRT, computer-generated images enable radiation doses to be "sculpted" to match precisely the shape of the tumor being treated, and to attack the tumor from several different angles. Because the technique is so accurate, higher doses of radiation can be used. In addition to potentially improving cure rates, the technique may lead to shorter treatment time for patients.

Recent studies done at New York's Memorial Sloan-Kettering Cancer Center show that the higher radiation doses possible with IMRT improved local tumor control almost 71%. Published reports also indicate a 13–35% improved patient survival rate. And, because IMRT treatment is faster and fewer complications result than from conventional therapy, patients are more able to continue to enjoy their normal lives as they undergo therapy.

Varian Medical Systems is currently the world's leading manufacturer of integrated radiotherapy systems that enable IMRT and other forms of radiotherapy treatment of cancer and other diseases. The company's oncology systems are composed of computerized medical linear accelerators, advanced software for processing diagnostic images and planning and delivering treatment, and specialized mechanical devices called multileaf collimators that shape the radiation beams to match the tumor. Studies are continuing to document the effectiveness of these products in treating prostate, head, neck, breast, pancreatic, lung, and other localized tumors.

In IMRT and other forms of radiotherapy tumor treatment, the medical linear accelerator is the key to delivering the radiation. Standing nearly nine feet tall and weighing 18,000 pounds, the accelerator speeds up electrons to 186,000 miles per

Varian Medical Systems engineers Chris Artig and Debi Salmon, with x-ray tubes. Tubes made by Varian Medical Systems are used in nearly one-half of the mammography systems and in nearly one-fourth of the CT scanners worldwide.

second (the speed of light) within approximately a meter of space. Once they reach this speed, the electrons collide with a metal target, which releases photons, or x-rays. When the photons hit human tissue, they produce highly energized ions that kill cells. Currently more than 4,200 of Varian's CLINAC® medical linear accelerators are treating thousands of patients around the world every day—in Memorial Sloan-Kettering Hospital, Moscow's Central Clinical Hospital, and Kyoto University Hospital in Japan, among many others. The company's Ximatron® simulators are also in widespread use, for localizing tumors and enabling medical staff to plot a detailed blueprint for radiotherapy treatment.

In addition to accelerators and simulators, Varian also provides a complete suite of integrated products, software, and support services: image acquisition software, for linking diagnostic images such as CT scans to the treatment planning process; treatment planning software; dynamic multileaf collimators; radiotherapy department information systems, for managing patients' complete care programs; and respiratory gating systems, which synchronize a patient's breathing pattern with the timing of radiation treatment beams.

One of the newest products in Varian's line of radiotherapy software and devices is called the SmartBeam IMRT QA. Co-developed with Radiological Imaging Technology, SmartBeam quality assurance software provides automated analysis of critical

PortalVision™ is Varian Medical Systems' all-digital system for taking "portal images" that are critical for positioning the patient and verifying the accuracy of the treatment. This system utilizes Varian's amorphous silicon flat-panel image-detection technology to create images during treatment, using the actual beam of the linear accelerator.

machine parameters, assuring that the radiation doses that are planned are exactly what are delivered. Accuracy measurements are taken at millions of different points and provided to the clinician in seconds, ensuring that patients receive their prescribed treatment. Analysis can even be performed on interrupted treatments, and registration is corrected to allow for patient movement. Varian leaders believe that the availability of SmartBeam software will enable many more hospitals and clinics to implement IMRT treatment programs.

All of these treatment components are combined in a single radiation therapy architecture or network that Varian calls its Generation Six System—the world's first and only fully integrated system from

a single supplier. The tools and services that are comprised in this system manage every part of a cancer treatment provider's program, from patient registration through treatment through oncology management. Generation Six streamlines the entire clinical process, eliminating redundant work and automating treatment delivery to provide efficient, more productive, and cost-effective service.

While 80% of Varian Medical Systems' products are focused on radiation cancer treatment, the company also holds the title of world's largest independent supplier of x-ray tubes for imaging in medical, scientific, and industrial applications. The company's X-ray Tube Products operation provides diagnostic tubes for the worldwide

diagnostic imaging industry, including tubes expressly designed for the most advanced mammography and computed tomography (CT) scanning applications. Varian's long-life tubes enable diagnostic systems to handle more procedures per hour and still maintain high image quality.

To remain at the forefront of medical diagnosis and treatment technologies, Varian Medical Systems operates the Ginzton Technology Center. Since its inception more than 40 years ago, this groundbreaking laboratory has contributed to pioneering work in such fields as medical imaging using ultrasound and CT scans, magnetic resonance imaging, night vision devices, and microwave integrated circuits. Currently the center is focusing on advancing Varian's Varisource® brachytherapy radiation systems, in which radioactive material is implanted directly in a tumor; digital x-ray imaging; and emerging biotechnologies. The center is also pursuing technologies and products that promise to improve disease management by using targeted energy to benefit molecular medicine.

In their corporate headquarters in Palo Alto, California, and in their manufacturing sites and sales offices worldwide, Varian Medical Systems' 2,300 employees are continuing their company's long history of pioneering innovation. As president and CEO Richard M. Levy affirms, the company's mission has been, and will continue to be, providing effective, cost reducing, and breakthrough solutions to the global medical community.

AGILENT TECHNOLOGIES

www.agilent.com

As its first annual report told readers, Agilent Technologies is a 60-year-old startup. From 1939 until 1999, the company was a core part of the world-renowned Hewlett-Packard Company. But in March of 1999, Hewlett-Packard announced that it was spinning off a separate company comprised of its test and measurement, semiconductor, health care, and chemical analysis businesses. The diversified technology company that resulted is Agilent Technologies.

Dave Packard (left) and Bill Hewlett developed an innovative audio oscillator in a Palo Alto, California, garage in 1939, used to test high-quality audio frequencies.

In just a few years, Agilent has become a global powerhouse in its own right. The company, whose headquarters are in Palo Alto, California, is already known as a major force in the design and manufacturing of test, measurement, and monitoring instruments as well as semiconductor and optical components. Agilent's 42,000 employees serve customers in more than 120 countries,

including many of the world's leading high-tech firms.

One of the key reasons for the great demand for Agilent's products and services is the steady transformation from analog to digital technology. Because digital components need greater degrees of precision than analog components and are powered by miniature circuitry, testing and measurement are even more critical to ensure reliable electronic products. Agilent's standard and customized equipment, systems, and software help to ensure such reliability in products' design, development, manufacture, and use. For example, printed circuit board engineers use Agilent tools to design their devices for efficient and cost-effective manufacturing and to validate that the products will perform as they should—in numerous configurations and environments. In the communications field, Agilent instruments evaluate network performance and identify problem areas, and monitor and manage network infrastructures to detect fraud and to troubleshoot service problems.

While Agilent is the world's largest test and measurement organization, it is also a leading supplier of advanced semiconductor products for communications and computer equipment makers. The company is a major source of fiber optic transceivers, which convert digital data into light signals for transmission over fiber optic cables, then convert the light signals back to digital form at the end of the communication. Agilent produces these transceivers for both local-area and wide-area networks. The firm also supplies

solid-state lasers for ultra-long-distance applications.

Agilent is a leading provider of life sciences and analytical instrument systems to scientists in life sciences, pharmaceutical, environmental, and chemical industries worldwide. The company offers scientists the range of instruments, systems, and services needed for success in acquiring and interpreting genetic and chemical information—from sample handling to analysis to data management and reporting. Agilent provides superior standards-based technology designed for maximum productivity, cost effectiveness, and ease in complying with regulatory requirements.

Agilent's health care solutions business is focused on helping customers improve the quality of patient care as well as keeping costs down. The company is a major provider of patient monitoring, cardiovascular ultrasound imaging, and critical-care information management systems. It is also the only technology provider of "point-of-care" diagnostic equipment for the full course of treatment, for example, continuous blood gas monitoring. One innovative product, the Heartstream ForeRunner™, has become standard equipment in many airplanes. The portable defibrillator, which can be used by non-medical people and is small enough to fit in a seat pocket, puts out a series of precisely timed, low-voltage impulses that can restore a traveler's heart rhythm in case of cardiac arrest.

All of Agilent's business sectors are tied together and supported by the

expertise of the researchers at the Agilent Technologies Laboratories. Discoveries made in this central research facility are applied to Agilent's businesses to create new products and markets and to provide new capabilities to their customers. Agilent scientists have made major contributions in the areas of DNA readers and cardiac ultrasound imaging, among many others. One recent product that resulted from work done at the center is a solid-state computer mouse that has no moving parts and uses an optical sensor for tracking.

Though a "newcomer," Agilent Technologies has quickly addressed both the opportunities and the challenges of its four core businesses. As Ned Barnholt, president and chief executive officer, points out, they are striving to live up to both their heritage and their potential.

Agilent's chemical analysis business collaborated with Caliper Technologies Corp. on these miniature laboratories called LabChip Kits. The Protein 200 LabChip Kits are used by chemists, biochemists, and molecular biologists to analyze proteins. The DNA 500 LabChip Kit automates the analysis of DNA fragments. Lab-on-a-chip technology integrates a large number of chemical manipulations on a single chip, speeding up chemical analysis, reducing cost, and enabling digital information to be shared.

SRI INTERNATIONAL

www.sri.com

The computer mouse. Hypertext editing. Halofantrine, a treatment for malaria. Magnetic ink character recognition for machine reading of bank checks. Laser radar for weather monitoring. An easy-clean oven surface.

What do these wide-ranging inventions have in common? They were all developed by SRI International, based in Menlo Park, California.

As company president and CEO Dr. Curtis Carlson explains, SRI International is in the "business of innovation." Since 1946, its staff members have been working to meet the challenges facing businesses, governments, and society at large. From its local roots, the organization has evolved into a worldwide concern involved in client-funded R&D, systems development, product development, consulting, and policy solutions. It is also moving some of its discoveries into the marketplace by spinning off technology companies.

One of its seven operating units, Information and Computing Sciences, is working toward creating technologies that provide better and more secure ways of gathering and sharing information. The group is developing natural language speech technologies for human-computer interaction, intrusion detection systems for networks, and new technologies for an intelligent Internet infrastructure. They are also creating software that will automatically translate speech into multiple languages.

Another division, the Information, Telecommunications and Automation Division, is developing secure wireless information systems, new technologies for better and faster package handling and sorting, artificial muscle technology, and an information-sharing system for managing a crisis or a military action. The division's Innovative Products team helps clients solve seemingly unsolvable product development problems. For example, when surgeons found it difficult to work with the awkward instruments used in the new field of minimally invasive surgery, the group was asked to address the problem. Their answer developed into a telepresence surgery system, which combines telerobotics, sensing, and 3-D imaging technologies. With this system, surgeons sit at a console using

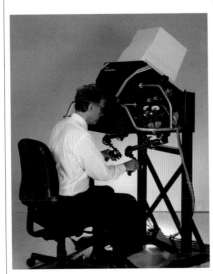

Surgeons are using SRI-developed instruments that incorporate robotics, sensing, and three-dimensional imaging technologies to perform minimally invasive surgery.

familiar tools whose actions are carried out robotically, instead of operating directly on a patient using difficult-to-manage equipment. The technology has been licensed to an SRI spin-off company, Intuitive Surgical.

SRI's Engineering and Systems Division provides solutions in the fields of electromagnetics and remote sensing, radio science and engineering, and systems development. The division tackles such challenges as developing ground-penetrating radar to locate land mines and using a large radio telescope to communicate with spacecraft.

The Physical Sciences Division addresses issues involving chemistry, physics, structural failure, and advanced materials. The team, for example, contributed to our understanding of the ozone hole; invented nonflammable, rechargeable batteries; and developed impact-resistant aircraft materials.

The Pharmaceutical Discovery and Biopharmaceutical Development Divisions assist government agencies, such as the National Cancer Institute, as well as commercial clients in developing and testing new drugs. Two agents the group has produced are vidarabine, an anti-virus drug, and tirapazamine, an anti-cancer drug that kills tumor cells that are the most resistant to treatment.

Research performed in SRI's Policy Division is aimed at providing clients with answers to their education, training, health, and human services problems. The division provides insight and information to improve the quality of life for people at home, at school, and

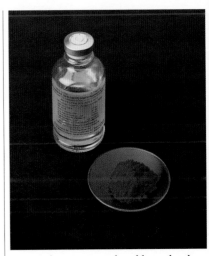

SRI's pharmaceutical and biotechnology research has resulted in promising anti-cancer agents and anti-HIV vaccines.

at work. One project has been California's "Healthy Start" program. The Policy group evaluated this major initiative that links health and social services to schools, and discovered that it has helped many families with food and clothing needs. Other studies underway include researching the causes and treatments for nicotine addiction and working with twins to learn more about the role of genetics in human health.

With its broad base in R&D, business management, and policy making, SRI International has produced a great number of solutions to the challenges facing people all over the world. And the new century may bring even greater opportunities for scientific discoveries and technological innovation. Currently the organization holds more than 800 patents and patent applications, and the number is growing. As it has in the past, SRI International is continuing to invent the future.

ACUSON CORPORATION

www.acuson.com

Ultrasound imaging, a technique that uses reflected sound waves that are beyond the limits of human perception to examine and diagnose internal body organs, took its first tentative steps in the world of medicine in the mid-1960s. Since that time, this non-invasive technology has been embraced by the medical community and become a critical tool in the war against disease.

Acuson Corporation, of Mountain View, California, has been for more than 20 years a leading provider of ultrasound systems that generate, display, archive, and retrieve ultrasound images. Acuson's products are used by hospitals, clinics, and private-practice physicians to make earlier and more accurate medical diagnoses than were previously possible.

Two of Acuson's most recent innovations, AcuNav™ and the Cypress™ Echocardiography System, are being touted by physicians as powerful new partners for diagnosing and treating heart and cardiovascular impairments. The AcuNav diagnostic ultrasound catheter actually enables physicians to visualize the heart from within. The device is inserted into a leg or neck vein, then maneuvered into the upper or the lower chamber of the right side of the heart. High-quality images and information about blood flow are then available, enabling life-saving procedures that doctors weren't able to perform before.

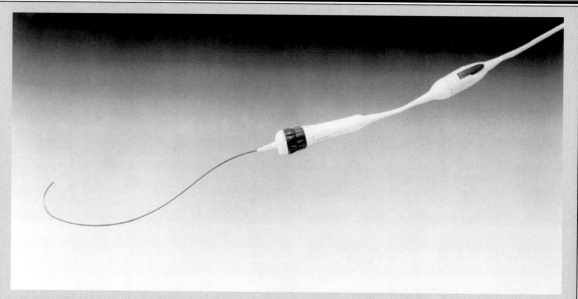

The AcuNav diagnostic ultrasound catheter from Acuson brings the full performance of medical ultrasound into the heart.

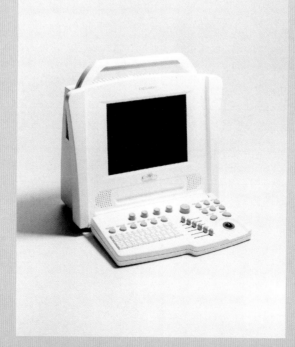

Acuson's Cypress Echocardiography System is a comprehensive cardiovascular product that also uses reflected ultrasonic waves to study the functioning of the heart. It is small in size and weighs less than 20 pounds, making it ideal for use in cramped patient-care areas and in mobile or remote facilities. And, just like Acuson's larger systems, it has the capacity to store patient exam information in high-resolution, digital format and to output that information to networks.

While these two products are providing breakthrough medical technology, Acuson's chairman and CEO Samuel H. Maslak affirms that the company won't be resting on its laurels. Acuson will continue to investigate new ultrasound applications and to provide new options and new features that will improve medical diagnostic capabilities.

Acuson's new Cypress Echocardiography System, weighing less than 20 pounds, is a comprehensive cardiovascular product.

COHERENT, INC.

www.cohr.com

When we think about light, most of us think about specific ways it helps us to live our lives. But light is actually unfocused and diffused—it's incoherent. Physicists and engineers, however, have learned how to control the power of light. Harnessed, or coherent, light can now be directed, focused, and used to benefit people in a great number of ways.

Coherent, Inc., headquartered in Santa Clara, California, is a pioneer in the field of laser technology. Lasers are devices that produce a coherent beam of light by causing atoms to radiate their energy in a special way. While they were only in their infancy when Coherent opened its doors in 1966, in the new millennium lasers have come of age. Lasers can now be found in virtually every part of the world, and bring their cutting-edge technology to scientific, medical, and consumer applications.

Coherent focuses its work in two different areas: medical and electro-optical. The company started providing products for the medical field in the

1970s, when it produced the first laser for use in ophthalmology, the branch of medicine that deals with the health of the eye. Since that time, Coherent has continued to develop lasers for use in medical procedures. Some current products are used as cutting tools in surgical applications, and others provide photodynamic therapy, or PDT, in which lasers activate drugs to achieve a therapeutic result. One of Coherent's new PDT lasers, called Opal Photoactivator™, treats a form of macular degeneration, the leading cause of blindness in people over 50. The company estimates that over 10 million people have had their sight saved through treatment with Coherent lasers.

In addition to ophthalmology, Coherent produces minimally invasive lasers for use in other medical fields, including orthopedics, urology, neurology, and oncology. The company also develops lasers for aesthetic applications, to help diverse populations look their best. Coherent's line of lasers includes products that treat wrinkles and resurface facial skin, remove tattoos and lesions, remove hair, and aid in cosmetic and reconstructive surgery. Compared with other treatment methods, lasers cause less bleeding and enable shorter hospital stays.

While Coherent's laser technologies serve a wide variety of medical needs, their electro-optical applications are even more numerous. In the scientific market, their lasers and precision optics equipment maximize research efforts in engineering, genetics, biology, chemistry, and physics. In the commercial arena, Coherent products are used in manufacturing and instrumentation.

When the Pathfinder Rover landed on Mars, people everywhere were treated to pictures of the Martian surface. But these photos wouldn't have been possible without the special cameras using optics manufactured by Coherent. Working with the Jet Propulsion Laboratory, Coherent fabricated a series of optics that were used in special equipment that acted as the headlights for the Rover as it made its way over the Martian terrain.

When it went into business more than 30 years ago, Coherent's breakthrough product was the first commercially available carbon dioxide laser. And while the company now produces lasers using several different technologies, including argon/krypton ion and diode-pumped solid-state lasers, the CO_2 laser is still a major contributor. Light from CO_2 lasers is absorbed readily by most nonmetallic materials. This makes such lasers good choices for cutting a wide range of organic and plastic materials, from acrylics to plywood

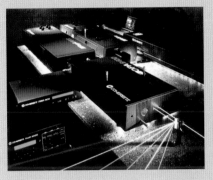

Ultrafast lasers: Coherent offers an extensive range of solid-state laser systems and accessories.

to cotton to silicon. Coherent's DIAMOND™ lasers can be set to cut through various material thicknesses, and, because they cut in pulses, the heat that occurs during processing is kept down. Industrial uses for these products include manufacturing, ceramic scribing, welding, and engraving.

Bernard Couillaud, Coherent's president and CEO, says that laser technology and precision optics will continue to find wider and wider applications in the new century; the last century was dominated by electronics, but the 21st century will be dominated by photonics, or light-related technology. Many of those applications will be in telecommunications, a field that Coherent recently entered with optical components that stabilize laser transmitters in networking products. While lasers have been used to cut and to remove, advances in the technology are now allowing them to enable. For lasers, and so many who benefit from them, the future is bright.

FOCUSING ON THE FUTURE: SILICON VALLEY RESEARCH

In the world of research, necessity, as the saying goes, is definitely the mother of invention. Once a need has been determined, you'll soon find a researcher hard at work to meet it. In Silicon Valley, researchers in industry, university settings, government centers, and applied research facilities are constantly testing theories and developing processes that advance the state of the art in the high-technology arena.

If you stop to think about it, nearly every electronics-related company that set down roots in the fertile environment of Silicon Valley did so because of an idea—an idea that the founders had to meet a need, and one that they researched and developed until it became reality. Early technology pioneers Russell and Sigurd Varian had the idea that they could use high-frequency energy to bounce off and locate aircraft and ships—the principle of radar. They researched and developed their idea in a Stanford University physics lab and eventually created a new electron tube they called the klystron, and a company called Varian Associates to produce it. Steve Wozniak and Steve Jobs wanted to develop a computer that would fit easily on a desktop and be simple for anyone to use. After studying every computer they came across, experimenting and tinkering, and

Opposite page: IBM's entry into the personal computer (PC) market in 1981 was viewed as the established business community's approval of a "fringe" technology.

A giant satellite dish on the Stanford University campus

sharing information with friends in the Home Brew Computer Club, they built one of their own, creating a product that led to the Macintosh line and enormously simplified interaction with computers. The company they established, Apple, grew from an idea, and from in-depth research and development.

Research facilities and researchers began making their mark in the area that would become Silicon Valley as early as 1939. In that year, leaders of the Ames Research Center, a government-run facility, broke ground in Sunnyvale, and went on to conduct research studies on everything from the problems of high-speed flight to the origins of life.

Following World War II, the Stanford Research Institute was founded in conjunction with Stanford University, and was dedicated to applying science to useful purposes. Working with innovative California businesses, SRI's initial efforts included developing a new plant source of rubber and developing solar collectors. Now known as SRI

International, the center has gone on to become a world-renowned research and development facility, particularly for the telecommunications industry.

IBM is another Silicon Valley giant whose research efforts have added enormously to the advancement of the electronics field. The area became home to an IBM research facility in 1952. At that lab, inventors and engineers worked together to develop a way in which large amounts of information could be stored in a computer so that any part of it would be available to the central processor very quickly. They created the RAMAC, which set in motion the disk drive storage industry. The lab, now called the IBM Research Center, is one of a number of IBM research facilities whose studies have led to improvements in photocopiers, laser printers, scanners, data storage systems, and Internet technologies.

One of the many renowned scientists with Silicon Valley roots was Palo Altan William Shockley. Shockley worked with other scientists and engineers to improve the transistor, the device that had replaced the problem-filled vacuum tubes used in early computers. Shockley headed an experienced research team at Shockley Semiconductor Laboratories

Russ and Sig Varian with their klystron, enabling pilots to "see" objects through fog and darkness.

and oversaw two colleagues at Bell Laboratories, with whom he shared the 1956 Nobel Prize in physics for developing the junction transistor. Many other Silicon Valley scientists have since joined Shockley as Nobel Prize winners for their extraordinary research efforts. These include Arthur Kornberg, who won the prize for his discovery of how DNA molecules are duplicated in the bacterial cell and for reconstructing the process in the test tube; Robert Hofstadter, who used a linear electron accelerator to measure and explore atomic nuclear structures; Kenneth Arrow, whose studies contributed to understanding welfare economics; and Henry Taube, who won for discoveries in the basic mechanism of chemical reactions.

Many other talented researchers have brought their considerable expertise to area facilities involved with medicine and matter. Carl Djerassi, a prominent figure in the development of the birth control pill, worked for Syntex Corporation, whose research lab was located at the Stanford Industrial Park. In 1962, in the foothills west of the university, leaders of the Stanford Linear Accelerator Center (SLAC) constructed a two-mile-long electron gun and began to probe the structure of matter at subatomic scale. SLAC's Richard Taylor shared the 1990 Nobel Prize in physics for his research involving the subatomic particles called quarks. Today

IBM's RAMAC—Random Access Method of Accounting and Control—the world's first random access computer. Its 100 circular disks were two feet wide.

T hose of us who are here now have a very difficult time placing confident bets on the development of this or that or the other science-based technology, and there's a lesson in there. It is that basic research, exploratory science, is terribly important, because you never really know what the next winner is going to be. Cambridge University, England, in 1855—if you had asked what its biology department would look like in 1880, you would have missed the Darwinian revolution. So we don't know exactly which of the things we're working on at Stanford today are going to be the ones that have terribly important relationships to human welfare, indeed, to human survival a hundred years from now.

Don Kennedy, Former President of Stanford University

Edward Ginzton at the Stanford Linear Accelerator Center (SLAC). Ginzton took over the job of building when Dr. William Hansen became ill. Ginzton later became a founder of Varian.

> I've been in T-bills for the last four years. I personally think that if you look at the rational price that's paid for performance, the multiple makes sense. Whenever the market goes up way past that, it goes back down as far as it went up. We weren't as far north in 1929 as we are today. So I'm assuming that they [stocks] are going to go down some day. (Interview conducted in 2000)
>
> **Larry Boucher,**
> **Founder of Adaptec**

SLAC is a national research laboratory with a staff of 1,300, operated by Stanford for the U.S. Department of Energy.

Another key Silicon Valley research center opened its doors to world-class scientists in 1970. Xerox Corporation's Palo Alto Research Center (PARC) charged its first team with the mission of creating "the architecture of information." PARC scientists promptly began meeting this goal by inventing numerous groundbreaking solutions, including collaborative tools, bit-mapped displays, object-oriented

Xerox Corporation's Palo Alto Research Center (PARC)

SETI@home is a scientific experiment that uses Internet-connected computers in the search for extraterrestrial intelligence (SETI).

programming, and client/server architecture. PARC scientists went on to develop many basic protocols of the Internet, and have contributed extensively to a wide range of computer-related fields.

In the 1980s, many of today's technology supercompanies started up in Silicon Valley to bring a product to market they believed would fulfill a need. One such company is Cisco Systems, whose premier product was developed out of a need to communicate. Cisco Systems founders Leonard Bosack and Sandra Lerner were frustrated by not being able to link their separate departments' computer networks at Stanford University. So they developed the network router, which became the key to connectivity, and cofounded the company that now produces a variety of

hardware products that form information networks.

Since the early '90s, the capabilities of the Internet have enabled research efforts to reach well beyond the confines of one company or one laboratory. Colleagues located in all corners of the planet now share ideas and information, focus on separate aspects of a single project, make use of varying technologies and sources, and support each other in their work. They can brainstorm in real time, and even view and discuss the same materials though they're separated by thousands of miles.

One example of an ongoing collaborative effort that makes extensive use of the Internet is the research relating to SETI—the Search for Extraterrestrial Intelligence. The answer to the question

"Are we alone in the universe?" is the focus of widespread study that began when microwave radio technology was first used to search for signals from other solar systems. Since that time, in the late 1950s, scientists and researchers in Russia and at the Ames Research Center, the Jet Propulsion Laboratory, the University of California Berkeley, the Planetary Society, and Ohio State University, among others, have all been involved in examining the possibilities of extraterrestrial life. Now, through the SETI@home project, anyone with an Internet-connected PC, researcher or not, can be part of the search effort. Affiliated with U.C. Berkeley's Project SERENDIP (Search for Extraterrestrial Radio Emission from Nearby Developed Intelligent Populations), SETI@home registers and connects computer owners and provides them with project software. When the owner's computer is idle, the software downloads 300 kilobytes of SERENDIP data and analyzes it. The results of the analysis are then sent back to the SERENDIP team, and used to help in the search for extraterrestrial

IBM's Almaden campus, San Jose, California—before the buildings

signals. As of February 2000, the SETI@home program had enlisted more than 1.6 million participants in 224 countries.

Still other research facilities are currently involved in a collaborative effort aimed at advancing semiconductor technology. Lawrence Berkeley National Laboratory, Lawrence Livermore National Laboratory, and Sandia National Laboratory have been working since 1997 with high-tech giants Intel, Advanced Micro Devices, and Motorola in an effort to find a way to pack many more transistors onto a single chip. Through this program, scientists and technicians recently developed a prototype that uses ultraviolet light to etch transistors onto semiconductors. It is hoped that this process will eventually allow chip makers to print faster, cheaper circuits that are well below 0.1 microns, a size that current technology probably won't be able to handle. The research consortium now includes IBM, Micron Technology, and Infineon Technologies.

As the capabilities of research programs continue to increase, some fear that scientists may be venturing into areas, such as animal cloning and technologies for weapons of mass destruction, that would be better left unstudied. As Albert Einstein stated after his research enabled the destructive force of the atomic bomb, "If only I had known, I should have become a watchmaker." But research can also lead to the cure for cancer, the end to hunger, and many other ways to benefit mankind. In Silicon Valley, research continues to thrive and to increase the reach of both people and technology.

uring the search to find a replicate hormone as a solution to female birth control, plant roots with natural steroids were harvested in the jungles of Mexico. ejandro Zaffaroni at Syntex, Mexico City, is sitting on the left.

A Short History of Silicon Valley

If one act can be singled out as the beginning of Silicon Valley, it might be Leland Stanford's decision to come to California. Trained as an attorney in Albany, New York, Stanford set up his new practice in Washington, Wisconsin, in 1848. After a fire destroyed his $3,000 legal library, Stanford left his practice and, in 1852, joined his brothers in merchandising to the gold miners in California. Though his new wife, Jane Lathrop Stanford, stayed behind in Wisconsin, she soon joined Stanford in California and became an integral partner in his success.

Once in California, Stanford became an early organizer of the Republican Party there. He ran unsuccessfully for state treasurer in 1857 and for governor in 1859. In 1860, he campaigned vigorously for Abraham Lincoln. In 1861, with Jane Stanford at his side, he campaigned statewide for governor and won decisively.

Together with fellow Sacramento merchants Collis P. Huntington, Mark Hopkins, and Charles Crocker, Stanford organized the Central Pacific Railroad Company (CPRR) to pursue the improbable idea of constructing a railroad across the Sierra Nevada mountain range. The U.S. government supported the project with land grants and loans, but the sums that were needed required Stanford and his partners to put up their entire fortunes.

Jane Lathrop Stanford

Leland Stanford

Leland Stanford, Jr.

Public displeasure over the seemingly impossible scheme echoed throughout the country. Adding to the argument, the California labor pool was composed primarily of former gold miners who demanded high wages and would abruptly leave their jobs at the news of a new gold strike. The 50-foot Sierra snowdrifts would make the railroad reliable only in summer. Railroad experts scoffed at the idea. And the cost of materials seemed prohibitive since they had to be shipped around South America or transshipped through the Isthmus of Panama.

One of the stories surrounding the building of the railroad was that by 1868 the company was running out of money; it seemed that the critics might be proven right. Though the rail line had reached Dutch Flat on July 4, 1866, and Cisco by that fall, the 1866–67 and 1867–68

Central Pacific Railroad

On May 10, 1869, the Central Pacific Railroad and the Union Pacific Railroad drew together in Promontory, Utah, as Leland Stanford wielded a sledge of Nevada silver to tap a spike of California gold into a polished laurel tie.

Palo Alto Railroad Station (circa 1898)

techniques they had learned in China. One was to be lowered by rope from the tops of cliffs and, while suspended, chip away at the granite and set explosives. Many lost their lives while setting the charges. Many froze to death. But by the spring of 1868, a great railroad tunnel east of Cisco had opened.

By the summer of 1868, 4,000 workers, two-thirds of whom were Chinese, had built the California Pacific Railroad over the Sierra. A Chinese crew was chosen to lay the final 10 miles of track, which were completed in only 12 hours. On May 10, 1869, trains of the CPRR and the westward-building Union Pacific Railroad drew together at Promontory, Utah. Leland Stanford wielded a sledge of Nevada silver to tap a spike of California gold into a polished laurel tie. The success of his railroad venture earned Leland Stanford and his partners the nicknames of the "Big Four" and "Robber Barons."

Construction workers during the building of Stanford University (circa 1890)

winters had been extremely difficult, and the working conditions near the summit hazardous. To complete the railway the CPRR would need 5,000 workers instead of the usual number of about 600.

Charles Crocker suggested bringing in Chinese laborers to finish the railroad. Chinese workers had already helped build the California Central Railroad, the railroad that ran from Sacramento to Marysville, and the San Jose Railway. When his idea was criticized because the workers were small in stature and not masons, Crocker replied, "The Chinese made the Great Wall, didn't they?"

At the low-for-the-times wage of approximately $28 per person per month, Chinese laborers were hired to do the most dangerous work of blasting out a roadbed and laying ties over the treacherous terrain of the high Sierra; after the first 23 miles, tracks had to be laid over rocky land that rose 7,000 feet in 100 miles. The workers used

Leland and Jane Stanford (on stage) at Stanford University's first day of classes in 1891

Their ownership in the Central Pacific Railroad brought the Stanfords enormous wealth. Leland Stanford also achieved additional political success when he became a U.S. senator in 1885 and was reelected in 1891. Additionally, the Stanfords bought thousands of acres of California land, including a famous 8,800-acre stock farm south of San Francisco, which became the future site of Stanford University. But tragedy devastated the family when the Stanfords' well-educated and talented son, Leland, Jr., died of typhoid at 15. After spending days at his deceased son's bedside, Leland Stanford drifted into a deep sleep. When he awoke he claimed that he had been visited by his son, who had said, "Father, serve humanity." This event gave birth to Stanford's idea of establishing Leland Stanford Junior University as a memorial to his son.

To run the school, Leland and Jane Stanford combed the country in search of talented professors and university administrators with philosophies similar to their own. The Stanfords believed that the true value of an education was in

I could lay down my life for the University . . . for the sincere hope I cherish in its sending forth into the world grand men and women who will aid in developing the best there is to be found in human nature.

Jane Lathrop Stanford, Co-founder of Leland Stanford Junior University

David Starr Jordan, first president of Stanford University

Trolley service in Palo Alto, California, ran down University Avenue from 1906 to 1925. (photo circa 1911)

The philosophy here has always been, way back before Terman to the time of David Starr Jordan, that if you have a good idea, and you have some potential for accomplishing human benefit, you ought to get it out there where it can be of practical use. This is a place that was formed at the time when the West was still a frontier. Practical knowledge was highly valued. Senator Stanford valued it highly, and the university has always had an affection for application as well as theory.

Don Kennedy, Former President of Stanford University

amount for the time. But Leland Stanford died only two years later. It was left to Jane Lathrop Stanford to keep the university running—through an economic depression, probate litigation, and a government claim of $15,000,000. Jane Stanford kept the young university afloat by selling numerous assets, including her personal jewelry and $500,000 worth of brandy. When she died in 1905, the university's financial affairs were in good order.

By 1910, the roots of Silicon Valley's technology future began to take hold. Dr. David Starr Jordan, who the Stanfords had selected to be the university's first president, had an early interest in science and technology. Jordan had been serving as president of the University of Indiana when the Senator and Mrs. Stanford came to call, delivered to Bloomington in their private railroad car.

learning practical skills that would be useful in the real world.

Leland Stanford Junior University was founded in 1891 with an endowment of over $20,000,000, an enormous

Stanford University's pioneer faculty

David Starr Jordan, first president of Stanford University

David Jordan remained president of Stanford for 21 years, and was responsible for recruiting a large part of the university's pioneering faculty. He lured outstanding teachers from Cornell University and other eastern campuses to create a high-powered science and engineering department that was to be the school's hallmark.

> The first real enterprise here was the old Mackay Radio. And that was started by a guy named Cyril Elwell. He started this company, bought the patents, came back and raised the capital while he was here. And it's interesting that David Starr Jordan encouraged some of his faculty to buy some of this stock, so you might say that [Jordan] was the first venture capitalist.
>
> **Bill Hewlett, Co-founder of Hewlett-Packard**

During his presidency, Jordan put $500 of his own money into a telephone and telegraph company begun in nearby Palo Alto by Cyril Elwell. Elwell initially called his firm the Poulsen Wireless Telephone and Telegraph Company, but a year later changed it to the Federal Telegraph Company. Within two years, Federal had become one of the largest firms of its kind in the country. In 1932, the company moved to New Jersey as Federal Electric and is today part of ITT.

In 1911, Lee de Forest was in San Francisco supervising the installation of his company's audion-based telegraph units on two U.S. Army transport ships. In the midst of it he learned that an officer of his New York–based company had drained the treasury and left de Forest broke and in debt. With no hope of saving his company, de Forest joined Elwell's company in Palo Alto. A year later he was arrested by federal marshals for stock fraud; he and the other officers of his failed firm were charged

Right: Federal Telegraph (circa 1918)

Below: High-tech switches at Federal Telegraph (circa 1925)

with deliberately misleading investors about a "queer little bulb" that was supposed to make it possible for people to talk with each other across the Atlantic Ocean. Federal Telegraph put up the $10,000 that kept de Forest out of jail until his trial, during which he was acquitted, though several other officers did go to prison. Three years later, engineers at American Telephone and Telegraph Company used de Forest's "queer little bulbs" to send radio messages from Arlington, Virginia, to the Eiffel Tower in Paris. De Forest's invention opened the way for a host of other firsts, from radio and television to radar and long-distance telephony, and earned him the title of "Father of Electronics."

De Forest's second home, Federal Telegraph, may have been the first incubator of Silicon Valley start-up companies. In 1913, two Federal employees, Peter Jensen and E. S. Pridham, left their jobs to start their own enterprise in the Napa Valley wine country north of San Francisco. There they invented the loudspeaker and founded a company called Magnavox. Not far away, a self-taught electronics genius from Idaho name Philo Farnsworth developed a device to focus and deflect an electron beam electromagnetically. This device, which was demonstrated in San Francisco in 1927, enabled the first all-electronic transmission of a picture and became the basis for television.

By the mid-1930s, Palo Alto and the surrounding area had become home to a small but bustling electronics industry and, along with it, the underpinnings of a unique infrastructure that would prove to be essential to the development of today's Silicon Valley. The most important feature of this emerging infrastructure was the connection between Stanford University and local technology enterprises: the school provided a steady stream of talented young scientists and engineers, as well as quite a bit of theoretical research, and the local employers provided jobs for graduates.

But when Federal Telegraph moved back east in 1931, an important source of local employment for young engineers disappeared. If a "community of technical scholars" was ever to be fully realized, the Valley needed a truly world-class company with strong roots in the region, a successful commercial electronics enterprise that would bring worldwide recognition to the area.

While other universities ignored the commercial sector, Stanford pursued alliances aggressively. Stanford President David Starr Jordan had invested his own money in Cy Elwell's company, and then promoted the venture to other faculty investors. When Fred Terman became the dean of the School of Engineering, he continued to forge the links between Stanford and local business.

When Leland Stanford gave his 8,800 acres to the university he had created, he included a proviso that prohibited the sale of any of that land, ever. During the late 1940s, this restriction presented a problem for university administrators. They were anxious to convert university land to cash

> I think a lot of people would like to think entrepreneurialism can be bottled up, that there's some secret sauce. Maybe it's like anything else: sometimes, when you have just a little bit of it, it's hard to describe. I think, in a very simple sense, it's the willingness to try something new, and to just keep at it. If I sat here and listed all my failures during my life, maybe you'd think I wasn't so entrepreneurial. But I think it's the style with which you approach something.
>
> **Carol Bartz, CEO, President, and Chairman of the Board of Autodesk**

so they could hire high-profile professors to enhance the school's academic prestige.

During his association with Stanford, Frederick Terman touted the virtues of cooperation between the university and developing technology industries. He, along with then-university president Wallace Sterling, came up with a plan that would both raise money for the school and enable the transfer of technology know-how from academia to the commercial marketplace. The pair's plan involved leasing land adjacent to the university to promising high-tech operations, a project that came to fruition as the Stanford Research Park. The proximity of the university to real-world industry created a powerful link between the two. Terman's innovative idea sparked a high-tech grass fire.

By 1939, the electronics industry was entering a period in which higher standards and more precise measurements were being demanded—something that former Stanford students William Hewlett and David Packard had been waiting for. As a graduate student, Hewlett had designed a device that produced controllable and accurate electrical signals at a predetermined frequency. He called the device an audio oscillator. He and Packard began a company in a rented Palo Alto garage to produce the oscillators, which could measure frequencies in the audible range and became invaluable to manufacturers of such products as loudspeakers.

Frederick Terman was a great believer in the commercial potential of the audio oscillator. Encouraging his former students, he helped to arrange a $1,000 bank loan to finance the pair's new venture. Years later Terman recalled that he could always tell how the young company was doing: "If the car was in the garage," he said, "there was no backlog. But if the car was in the driveway, business was good."

In 1940, a small group of physicists

> A couple of words of advice: One is be very careful about the people you select. Their fit with your culture, values, and fundamental beliefs is very important. Also, things will probably take twice as long and will be twice as difficult as you think they're going to be. So you need to be prepared and have staying power.
>
> **Dr. Mihir Parikh, Founder of Asyst Technologies**

working at Stanford University announced the invention of a device that utilized two electromagnetic resonators in a vacuum tube. The device swept ultra-short radio waves across the sky in an invisible beam, reflecting an "echo" from any solid object. This "klystron," invented by brothers Russell and Sigurd Varian and their colleague William Hansen, was light and relatively energy efficient. During the Second World War, it was used to detect Nazi U-boats that had come to the surface for oxygen during the night. The destruction of the U-boat fleet allowed American cargo and troop ships to reach England; the Varians' invention provided the advanced technology needed to turn the tide of the war in Europe. In 1948, the klystron tube became the cornerstone of the company the brothers and several colleagues founded in San Carlos, just north of Palo Alto—Varian Associates.

The usefulness of the klystron tube transcended its wartime applications. In the ensuing years, it helped make commercial air navigation safe, opened the possibility of worldwide communications via satellites, and led to the development of high-energy

---

> If any one person could be considered the sort of seminal character for the Silicon Valley it was certainly Fred Terman. Terman decided to buy and sell a chemistry department . . . one doesn't do this often.
>
> **Carl Djerassi, Father of the Birth Control Pill**

> An interesting thing about Silicon Valley today is convergence. Convergence of computers and communications, television and telephone. But the original convergence, you might say, was Silicon Valley itself. You had the convergence of Stanford University and other institutions of higher learning. You had the convergence of Bill Hewlett and Dave Packard and the Varian brothers and their entrepreneurial efforts. Their being wildly successful impressed other companies to consider locating here. And then you had the convergence of this incredible climate and all of the people that it attracted.
>
> **Fred Hoar, Former Marketing Director of Apple**

---

particle accelerators useful in medicine and nuclear physics. At Stanford, a two-mile linear accelerator used klystrons to power atom-smashing research.

Varian Associates was the first company to move into the Stanford Research Park in 1954. Hewlett-Packard came soon after, joining Varian as the nucleus of the park. During the 1950s, large national electronic corporations began to establish a real presence in Silicon Valley, including Admiral, General Electric, Sylvania, Kaiser, General Precision, and Lockheed.

IBM had first come to the Valley in 1952. The company had sent a small group of engineers and scientists out west to set up a research laboratory in San

Dr. Fred Terman

Jose, to engage in research and the production of data-processing systems and computer components. Eventually, that little group invented the disk drive.

By the late 1960s, Lockheed Aircraft Corporation's Research Laboratory in Palo Alto and its Missiles and Space Company in nearby Sunnyvale were employing 26,000 people. The Cold War and the space race would fuel high technology with tax dollars.

After being awarded the Nobel Prize in 1956 for his work on the transistor, William Shockley sent the word out that he was looking for the best people available to work at his new company. With the help of his former Cal Tech chemistry professor, Arnold O. Beckman, Shockley received financial backing. Since Beckman's southern California–based medical instruments company, Beckman Instruments, had a division at the Stanford Research Park, Shockley Semiconductor was set up nearby.

Shockley's reputation as one of the country's most brilliant physicists preceded him, and the announcement that he was hiring engineers and scientists for his new enterprise produced a deluge of applications—the cream of the electronics world. But for all the brilliance that Shockley brought to the world of science, he lacked terribly in people skills and common sense. David Packard recalls Shockley coming to him for advice on how to hire a secretary and where to buy pencils. His bright young research team felt his management style overbearing. He employed lie detector tests, second-guessed his staff, and had the acutely annoying tendency to talk

> B ut the war [WW II] changed all that, the war made electronics a universal commodity. And that's when things really started to happen.
>
> **Bill Hewlett, Co-founder of Hewlett-Packard**

> I t's about being at the right place at the right time, and essentially, we were there. We didn't know it at the time, but that's what happened, because we decided to concentrate on electronic instruments. Fred Terman and Bill and I had a sort of game. [Terman] would invite these people out to tell them about what a great place this was going to be and then he'd send them over to see us and we'd back him up on that. It was kind of the old one-two punch.
>
> **Dave Packard, Co-founder of Hewlett-Packard**

down to employees as though they were children.

By late 1957, seven of Shockley's stars, Dick Grinich, Jean Hoerni, Gordon Moore, Sheldon Roberts, Julius Blank, Jay Last, and Eugene Kleiner, were looking seriously for a way out. They were determined to stay together as a group, but no company was willing to hire them all, so they decided to start a company of their own. Venture capital was scarce

> A lot of really big companies have great scientific products that are just not ready for market yet. We licensed a core technology from AT&T and actually took it and built up a sellable application. We proved to them that there was a real business in it, and sold it back to them.
>
> **Michael D. Metcalf, Founder of Sound Advantage**

Dave Packard (on right) during Hewlett-Packard's early years

on the West Coast at the time, so the young scientists called on Kleiner's uncle's New York City–based investment house for help in finding companies interested in investing in a semiconductor operation. The firm assigned Arthur Rock to help arrange venture funding for the fledgling company.

Fairchild Semiconductor was founded in 1957 by Shockley's Traitorous

Sigurd Varian (driving a motorcycle with a sidecar and an unidentified woman and dog)

> **I**n the next half century, people will see as well as hear around the world. Pocket-sized radio instruments will enable individuals to communicate with anyone, anywhere. Newspapers, magazines, mail, and messages will be sent through the air at lightning speeds and reproduced in the home.
>
> **Robert Sarnoff, Radio and Television Pioneer, in a Speech Made in 1949**

Eight, and backed by industrialist Sherman Fairchild, a 60-year-old industrialist, inventor, pioneering aviator, and entrepreneur with the foresight to recognize the potential of the infant microelectronics industry. He invested half a million dollars.

To complete their team, the seven scientists called on Robert Noyce, who had remained with Shockley, to join the new company as its general manager. Noyce didn't need much convincing;

Dr. William Hansen, pioneer of nuclear induction devices

though he was Shockley's golden boy, he was as disillusioned as his colleagues were. The eight submitted their resignations all at once, which stunned and enraged Shockley. He would forever refer to his former employees as "the Traitorous Eight."

Fairchild Semiconductor became the leader in most fields that it pioneered; during the 1960s, the opportunities in semiconductors appeared endless. However, struggles within the company and the departure of many of its

I t was in January 1952. IBM had selected me and asked me to report out here almost immediately. The reason they sent me out to California was to open a laboratory on the West Coast. I was given complete freedom to select the projects and to select the staff, which was the kind of freedom I thought was rare, and so I took the job with great enthusiasm.

By using tapes, tape loops, drums, plates, rods, and even wires to randomly select the data that was recorded, we put these through intellectual simulation. And out of that came the decision to go to disks. A large disk, which was two feet in diameter, ended up as the choice. It's flat, and information can be obtained rapidly on its surface, on each side, and you can go up and down a stack of them. We stacked 50 of them, so we had 100 surfaces.

Reynold Johnson, IBM Inventor of the Computer Disk Drive

talented and high-profile leaders took their toll. Fairchild Semiconductor is now just a shadow of its former self.

Fairchild Semiconductor spawned a generation of entrepreneurs unique in world history. By the early 1970s, former Fairchild employees had started 41 semiconductor companies. In describing the spin-offs from Fairchild, a local trade-paper editor for the first time dubbed them "Silicon Valley," after the main ingredient in the semiconductor. By 1966, the Valley was reported to have the largest concentration of microelectronics companies in the world.

In 1968, Bob Noyce and Gordon Moore joined with process-development expert Andrew Grove and left Fairchild to start another enterprise. With the help of venture capitalist Art Rock, they raised

I think one of the things that is least effective in encouraging creativity is to give the impression that the student so often gets in school, that all of the nice things, the important things are found out nicely and neatly. It has been my experience that everything, including all of the more difficult inventions I've made—I counted recently and I find I have some 85 issued patents, which makes me at least close to being in the major league on numbers—requires many failures to accomplish. To do creative work, one must overextend oneself. One must count on falling on his face.

William Shockley, Nobel Laureate

$5 million in start-up money. Rock raised the capital in 30 minutes over the telephone. When the new company, Intel, was founded, they decided to focus on memory. It was a little-contested area of the market.

When Intel's Ted Hoff's invention of the microprocessor was announced in 1972, it wasn't clear that it would lead to the development of the personal computer.

But Hoff's remarkable invention, nursed into silicon by Federico Faggin, made it possible to produce computers that were much smaller and much cheaper. For only a few thousand dollars, virtually anyone could have a computer.

T he transistor is an amplifying element that was invented at Bell Laboratories in the late 1940s. The Bell Labs at that time had a major project led by Bill Shockley. But the project team included John Bardeen and Walter Brattain and Gerald Pearson and other people, each of whom in his own right was known to be a first-class scientist.

Jim Gibbons, Former Dean of Engineering of Stanford University

The video game revolution was started in 1972 by a 26-year-old Ampex research engineer named Nolan K. Bushnell. Bushnell set up shop in his

William Hansen at the Ryan High Voltage Labs, Palo Alto, California

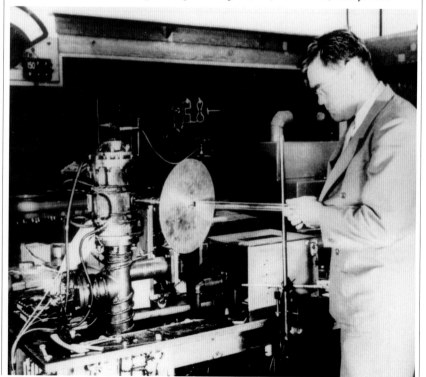

University Avenue, Palo Alto, California, circa 1895

Santa Clara home in one of his daughter's bedrooms. Within two years Bushnell's company, Atari, had sold more than 10,000 electronic Pong games, which provided powerful competition to pinball machines, pool tables, and board games. It was a change that would remake amusement arcades everywhere. In 1977, Warner Communications acquired the company for about $30 million, with Bushnell receiving half. With his big "cash-in," Bushnell completed the image of the high-tech entrepreneur, replacing forever the idea that founders who built companies stayed with them from birth to death.

The founding of Apple Computer and the emergence of the personal computer were the next "big things" to hit Silicon Valley during the late 1970s. Apple's two founders were Steve Jobs and Steve Wozniak. The two Steves struck up a friendship that led to their first commercial enterprise together. They both wanted to buy an Altair computer kit, but neither could afford one.

Venture capitalist Don Valentine

> We were trying to make the transistor—that was his original objective. Dr. Shockley thought that he could make an inexpensive silicon transistor and set up the company to pursue that goal. And while he had the fantastic physical intuition about what was going to go on in the materials and what the physics of the structure we were building was going to be, he had some peculiar ideas on how to motivate people.
>
> **Gordon Moore, Founder of Intel**

Jean Jones, Robert Noyce, and Gordon Moore at Jones's desk, circa 1970

We have a slogan at Autodesk called "Fail Fast Forward." What that is saying is, failure is fine; just make sure you quickly identify it when something's not working, and hope that at least it was a forward step. Even half a step is fine. Then try something else, and let's go.

Carol Bartz, CEO, President, and Chairman of the Board of Autodesk

didn't invest when he met Jobs and Wozniak, but he did give them some good advice. He told the two young entrepreneurs to get themselves an experienced business manager, and he put them in touch with one of the most important contacts they would make for the future of their company: Mike Markkula.

During the 1980s, Japanese manufacturers took away Silicon Valley's

I came out to California. That was the first time I'd ever been in California. That was '57, and we agreed to form a company, and then go around to various corporations and try and raise the million and a half dollars which they felt they needed.

Art Rock, Venture Capitalist

And we sat down, literally sat down with the *Wall Street Journal*, and went through all of the companies on the New York Stock Exchange to identify those that we thought might be interested in a semiconductor operation. We identified some 32 companies, and the investment bankers went out and talked to all 32. And all 32 turned the idea down. And then, quite by accident, they ran into Sherman Fairchild, who really was a technology buff. He loved new technology—he had originally set up a company to do aerial surveying, and he had to make both an airplane company and a camera company to have everything he needed to do the aerial surveying. His apartment was full of all the latest electronic gadgets. He introduced the investment bankers to the chairman of Fairchild Camera and Instrument, and they took a look at the group and decided they were willing to risk a modest investment to see if we could do anything. So, we got caught up with Fairchild, and that was the formation of Fairchild Semiconductor.

Gordon Moore, Founder of Intel

commodity memory-chip market with superior quality and cutthroat pricing. The largest Valley semiconductor makers dropped out of the competition and focused on microprocessors, which turned out to be a blessing in disguise.

The early eighties proved to be a

Stanford University Marching Band. Always irreverent, a show by itself.

good time for entrepreneurial startups. Among them were Sun Microsystems, Intuit, Asyst Technologies, Adobe Systems, and Cypress Semiconductor. Though Cold War money was slowly drying up, venture capital was replacing military dollars.

When IBM joined the personal computer revolution in 1981, Apple Computer advertised that they welcomed IBM as a competitor. IBM's freely licensed technology would soon dominate the personal computer market. And the company's agreement with Microsoft Corporation to supply the software platform for IBM PCs would make Microsoft's founder, Bill Gates, the world's richest man. The world's acceptance of the personal computer in business increased the efficiency of commerce exponentially. Many occupations became obsolete because most small businesses could function

more efficiently without as many secretaries, typists, operators, and receptionists. Using a personal computer, the average worker's production increased dramatically. Silicon Valley prospered.

Before the advent of the personal computer, a computer-based communications network by the name of ARPANET existed between academia and the government. The Internet slowly opened up to the public. As AOL pioneered the global village concept, Netscape came on like a tornado. In 1994, Netscape, a Silicon Valley company established by former Silicon Graphics founder Jim Clark and Marc Andreessen, inventor of one of the early Internet search engines called Mosaic, offered a consumer-friendly way to search the growing Internet .

On the heels of the end of the Cold War, in 1992, the Internet began to open up to the general public. The Internet's

popularity was dependent on several technologies coming together. The convergence of affordable personal computers, cheap RAM (memory), powerful microprocessors and multi-protocol routers that allowed different computer systems to communicate with one another all were necessary for the Internet's rapid growth.

As AOL pioneered the global village concept, Netscape's Internet browser came on like a tornado. Netscape, a Silicon Valley company founded by former Silicon Graphics founder Jim Clark and Marc Andreessen, inventor of one of the early Internet search engines called Mosaic, offered a consumer-friendly way to browse the growing Internet. With Netscape immediately dominating the emerging Internet browser market, major American companies were eager to get on the bandwagon. Microsoft soon entered the market and eventually captured Netscape's lead. Netscape was acquired by AOL in 1998.

In 1995, David Filo and Jerry Yang incorporated a company called Yahoo!. With Yahoo!'s tremendously successful initial public offering, the Internet bubble began. Most national economies were soon filled with fledgling dotcoms, firms started primarily for Internet business.

With the Internet boom, hundreds of new ventures without profitable business plans were financed with billions of dollars. As a result, hundreds of old Silicon Valley service businesses, including restaurants and small grocers, closed their doors as rents went up.

The rush to Silicon Valley was

contagious. Cutting-edge technology and the new "gold rush" attracted people from all over the world. One of the most important addresses for the new e-commerce–styled businesses was Palo Alto, California. Rents began to exceed downtown Manhattan and Tokyo. And in early 2000, signs began to surface that the profitable aspect of the Internet wasn't going to be as lucrative as anticipated.

In 2001, economic restructuring began. Technology stocks began a long dive. Layoffs around the world, particularly in Silicon Valley, became commonplace. A common sign in windows read "For Lease." The bubble had burst.

The world's security was shaken by terrorists in New York City and Washington, D.C., on September 11, 2001. With America and its allies preparing for a long, protracted war against terrorism, the future is unclear. However, technology offers hope, not only in defeating an enemy but also in reaching distant ears with reason. Silicon Valley's economy has always been boom and bust, but the real value it has given the world is its ability to invent and apply technology. That process is continuing. High-technology companies that downsized are still inventing new ways to improve the world. The rebirth is already under way.

John McLaughlin, President of the Institute for the History of Technology

IBM CORPORATION

www.ibm.com

Though most Silicon Valley companies got their start sometime in the 20th century, there aren't many whose origins date back to the 19th century. IBM is one of those. In 1888, in New York, Harlow and Willard Bundy started a business based on Willard's invention of a clock that could record the arrival and departure of workers—the time clock. A few years later, Bundy Manufacturing became the International Time Recording Company, which later became part of the Computing-Tabulating-Recording Company of America. Because of the new equipment the company continued to add to its line, in 1924 C-T-R adopted the name International Business Machines Corporation.

IBM's history of innovation is just as long as its company history. Following the success of the time clock, the company developed the punch-card calculator, the electric typewriter, the large-scale calculating computer (which was 50 feet long and 8 feet high), and FORTRAN, a computer language for technical work. It also produced the first high-speed cache memory for computers, which made prioritized information available much faster. And it developed the concept for the relational database, in which information is stored in computers arranged in easy-to-interpret tables, and on which nearly all databases today are based. Among other IBM innovations are the computer architecture known as RISC (Reduced Instruction Set Computer), which boosts computer speed by using simplified instructions for frequently used functions; and the first million-bit memory chip, which was twice as fast as the previous chip but took up a third of the space.

As IBM grew and developed new products, it also spread from its home in New York to San Jose, California, as well as to offices and plants throughout the world. Its first Santa Clara Valley facility was a punch-card manufacturing plant, which was soon followed in 1952 by a major research lab in San Jose. There researchers investigated new methods for storing large amounts of data that could be available to a central processor in just milliseconds. After four years the Random Access Method of Accounting and Control (RAMAC) was born, and

with it the beginning of the disk drive storage industry.

That first research lab is now known as the IBM Almaden Research Center, and is one of eight laboratories worldwide that make up IBM Research. Since its first effort to develop the hard-disk drive, the lab has concentrated on advancing IBM's future by adding to the fundamental scientific understanding of emerging technologies, and by working with product developers to create and improve products. Almaden scientists demonstrated for the first time that an organic material could be used as a photoconductor, which led to IBM's first photocopier and later to a laser printer. Their pioneering of computational methods for quantum chemistry has led to a better understanding of the electronic structure of atoms and molecules. Their work with holography—in which light is manipulated to create three-dimensional images without a camera—led to the invention of the Checkout Scanner™, which is found in supermarkets nationwide. And the revolutionary instrument they developed, known as the Scanning Tunneling Microscope™, produced the world's first image of atoms on a surface. Now the center is focusing on database improvements, data storage systems and software, content- and knowledge-management tools, human-computer interface improvements, Internet technologies, and research in computer science theory. In 1999 alone IBM took out over 2,700 U.S. patents.

All of this is certainly a long way from the development of the time clock. As it has grown in size and maturity, IBM has also grown with the times, and is now a leading force in the development and manufacture of advanced information technologies. Since 1997 the company has been shifting toward forwarding e-business applications and solutions, and is now concentrating on services, software, and component technology. In addition to being able to buy IBM-produced products, people are now also able to experience the benefits of IBM expertise through other companies' branded products, the infrastructure of the Internet, and through IBM's consultancies and services.

One important Internet product that IBM has developed is WebSphere™, a universal Internet software platform that

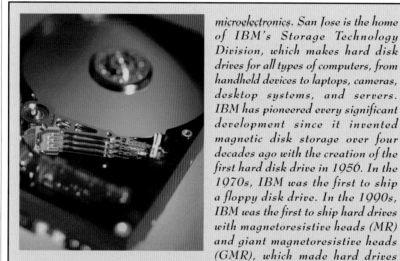

IBM develops and manufactures the industry's most advanced information technologies, including computer systems, software, networking systems, storage devices, and microelectronics. San Jose is the home of IBM's Storage Technology Division, which makes hard disk drives for all types of computers, from handheld devices to laptops, cameras, desktop systems, and servers. IBM has pioneered every significant development since it invented magnetic disk storage over four decades ago with the creation of the first hard disk drive in 1956. In the 1970s, IBM was the first to ship a floppy disk drive. In the 1990s, IBM was the first to ship hard drives with magnetoresistive heads (MR) and giant magnetoresistive heads (GMR), which made hard drives faster and more reliable and gave them higher capacity. In 1999, IBM introduced the world's highest capacity hard drives for notebooks, desktop PCs, and server systems.

IBM Microdrives are compact, high-capacity, high-performance removable storage for personal, portable, and handheld electronic devices. The world's smallest and lightest hard disk drives hold up to 340 megabytes on a one-inch-diameter disk that weighs only 0.7 ounce. That's enough capacity to store 1,000 photographs compressed or 1,000 novels. NASA astronauts successfully stored and brought back digital images on IBM's revolutionary one-inch hard disk drive during the recent Atlantis and Discovery shuttle missions.

can support any kind of e-business and makes deploying applications faster. The company also runs a comprehensive Web hosting business and offers network computing services to smaller customers. With Vodafone AirTouch, IBM is designing and building an Internet portal that will allow businesses and individuals to access content and services over the Internet using a wireless device. And because all e-business applications reside on servers, IBM is manufacturing

new Netfinity servers based on Intel processors to ensure reliability and provide the greatest memory capacity possible. To ensure reliability of e-business transactions, IBM has also established an e-business testing center. Here the company models customers' technology infrastructures, then stress tests them to see if they can handle the required load.

While IBM's first PC, introduced in 1981, was an immediate success, chairman and CEO Louis Gerstner, Jr., believes that the era of the traditional PC is over. Computing power is now moving to the network, he states, and the PC will be transformed into a number of specialized computing devices. One of IBM's innovations in this area is the electronic newspaper, which can be downloaded and printed for reading. Another is a wearable, belt-mounted PC that features a tiny headset-mounted

display, a storage device, and speech recognition software. With this package, wearers can access computer drawings, enter information by voice, and submit digital records without using their hands. IBM also develops "post-PC" processors—faster, adaptable chips that are needed in advanced communications products.

Despite its expanding focus, one area in which IBM continues its long-term work is in disk storage. In June of 1999, the company introduced the world's smallest hard disk drive. The IBM Microdrive™ can store up to 1 gigabyte of data on a disk the size of a U.S. quarter. This means that it can hold a thousand high-resolution photos or a thousand 200-page novels. The Microdrive can be found in a variety of handheld electronic devices, including digital cameras, handheld PCs, and video cameras. The first 1-gigabyte hard

Artwork highlights the beautiful countrified Almaden campus in San Jose, California.

drive, which was introduced in 1980, was the size of a refrigerator and weighed 550 pounds. It also cost $40,000.

Because the advent of e-commerce has so changed the dynamics of doing business, another area in which IBM is providing its expertise is in consulting services. In fact, IBM Global Services is now the world's largest information technology services provider. The 138,000 professionals who consult for IBM in 160 countries help customers learn about and work with the new business models. The company's network of e-business Innovation Centers also provides clients with experts who can assist with interactive design, Web use analysis, and data mining technologies. The IBM Small Business WebConnection service helps small businesses get up and running on the Internet by providing domain name registration, business-class e-mail, data transaction security, and technical support.

With its new focus on the Internet and e-business, IBM has shown itself to be not only a 19th- and 20th-century survivor but a continuing leader in the world marketplace. And with its ability to transform itself and drive change, the company expects to meet the challenges of the new century and continue to supply ever-expanding markets with reliable, high-performance, and innovative goods and services. IBM has grown from a small business machinery company to a full-fledged, state-of-the-art information technology leader. In fact, *Business Week* magazine recently called it "The biggest dot.com of them all."

INTEL CORPORATION

www.intel.com

Intel Corporation, headquartered in Santa Clara, California, has a long history of innovation and growth. It was in 1968 that Chairman of the Board Andrew Grove joined Robert Noyce and Gordon Moore to found the company focused on an overlooked part of the computer-chip industry: memory. Since that time, Intel has grown from a one-room office housing 12 employees to a $29 billion company of 70,000 strong. Along the way it has helped to revolutionize the way computers handle information.

During its first 15 years, Intel pioneered the development of semiconductor memory products. This included the first dynamic random access memory (DRAM) and the first erasable programmable read-only memory (EPROM). But during that time Intel also developed the world's first microprocessor. This breakthrough invention—an integrated circuit formed on a tiny piece of silicon—could

Research and development operations are major factors in Intel's domination of the world chip market.

regulate electrical current and control the processing of data in a personal computer. Building on the promise of this remarkable achievement, Intel eventually began to transform itself from a semiconductor memory company to a microcomputer company. Today it continues to grow and evolve, developing and manufacturing the chips, circuit boards, systems, and software that go into advanced computing systems.

Intel may be best known for its line of Pentium® microprocessors, including its newest generation, Pentium III microprocessors. While microprocessors can be found performing useful functions in everything from space shuttles to coffee makers, the powerful Pentium processor allows computers to more easily incorporate "real world" data, such as speech, sound, and handwriting. It does its work quickly—Pentium processors can execute up to several million instructions per second. Intel's first microprocessor, the 4004, contained 2,300 transistors, or current controllers, to do the job. One current line of Pentium processors boasts 5.5 million transistors, enabling speedy computer-aided design, mechanical engineering, and scientific computation. Another line, of 7.5 million-transistor processors, rapidly processes video, audio, and graphics data. Its accompanying high-speed memory chip lets computer users capture, edit, and share digital photos with friends and family over the Internet. Users can also edit or add music to home movies. And with a video phone they can send video over the regular phone line or the Internet.

Intel Pentium IV processor and Intel 850 chipset

Intel's Pentium III processors have been designed to enhance the Internet computing experience. These processors enable such applications as data visualization and speech recognition, as well as top-of-the-line audio, video, graphics, and animation. A new line of desktop processors, code-named Willamette, is expected to provide the fastest mainstream microprocessors in the industry, at least 1.5 gigahertz. Willamette processors will integrate both graphics and memory, and offer enhanced performance features. With every new generation of processors, Intel is enabling greater and greater speed and capability.

While Intel is committed to continuing to develop ever more powerful microprocessors, for both entry-level and high-end systems, it also designs and manufactures other products for use in computing and networking. Its chipsets—chips, or integrated circuits, that work as a unit to support microprocessors—perform essential computer logic functions. Its flash memory products provide easily programmable memory for computers,

mobile phones, and other chip-based devices. This kind of memory also retains data when power to the unit is turned off. Intel's embedded control chips increase performance in automobile braking systems, laser printers, and cellular phones.

Intel's networking products are helping business people everywhere to work more productively and manage their work more easily. For example, the company's hardware and software quickly enable many of the unseen but necessary jobs the click of a networked mouse can set in motion. These include compression and decompression of downloaded material; encryption, or the encoding of data to prevent unwanted access; security checking; and scanning

Robert Noyce, Intel's founder. Noyce died of heart failure in 1992, at the age of 65.

for viruses. Their products are also enabling greater and better use of the Internet, delivering data from the World Wide Web to desktops by way of powerful servers. Intel switches, hubs, and routers also speed up information access.

One of Intel's goals is to continually expand the capabilities of personal computers and enable more and more people to be part of the "connected" world. To reach that goal, they are leading or participating in a number of industry initiatives. These cooperative projects aim to bring new features and uses to Intel computing systems, for example, to enable personal computers to go from "deep sleep" to full power in five seconds, and to let users connect dozens of peripherals—from joysticks to speakers—through one port.

One of these projects is known as the Wired for Management (WFM) Initiative. This initiative was begun to reduce the costs of owning a personal computer by developing a new generation of desktop, server, and mobile systems that can be managed over a network. Working with other industry leaders, Intel

Gordon E. Moore, Intel's founder and current chairman emeritus of the board

is helping to establish guidelines that will let management programs communicate with any WFM-compliant system. Mobile computer manufacturers will be able to build on these guidelines to provide better mobile computer performance, such as constant monitoring of system health and lower power consumption.

Another project under development is the Visual Computing Initiative. This initiative is designed to speed up the growth of visual computing, in which 3-D graphics, video, and digital imaging technologies combine to deliver interactive, life-like computing experiences. Other visual computing efforts are under way to improve the editing and sharing of digital pictures on PCs and to bring arcade-quality games to PCs.

A third initiative, the Internet Health Initiative, is helping doctors and their patients put the Internet to greater use. Working with the American Medical Association and other health-care leaders, Intel is assisting in making Internet technology more available. With this technology, doctors can automate routine communications with their patients, leaving more time for in-person

visits and care. Through the Internet, patients can have access to vast amounts of health-related information.

As one of the world's leading technology companies, Intel is very committed to science, math, and technology education. Over the years, the company has contributed over $100,000,000 to colleges and universities, elementary and secondary schools, and community organizations. Through a large number of programs, Intel is working to increase awareness, understanding, and use of technology.

Located in the heart of Silicon Valley, the Santa Clara site is Intel's corporate headquarters.

For example, its Teach to the Teachers program is helping more than 40,000 science teachers learn how to better teach the subject. Its Computer Clubhouse program is helping inner-city children become computer literate on the most up-to-date computers. Intel is also working to encourage women and minorities to pursue science and engineering careers. In addition the company sponsors two important high school science competitions: the Intel Science Talent Search and the Intel

International Science and Engineering Fair.

With its extensive research and development efforts, Intel is taking its long history of innovation into the future. It is also fulfilling its mission to become the "preeminent building block supplier to the worldwide Internet economy." Today, the number one reason people buy personal computers is to be able to get on the Internet. Intel's Andrew Grove believes that this interest in the Internet is increasing the demand for computing performance by a factor of 10, and that faster and more powerful processors will be necessary to meet that demand. Intel's vision is to provide the chips that will connect a billion high-performance PCs around the world.

Andy Grove, Intel's founder and chairman

SIEMENS AG

www.usa.siemens.com
www.siemens.de

You couldn't call Siemens AG a newcomer to the world of innovation—the company has been designing, developing, and manufacturing electrical engineering and electronic systems for over 150 years. And you couldn't say that Siemens is focused on just a small segment of the marketplace—the company provides products and services that advance energy and automation solutions, information and communications, health care, transportation, building technologies, microelectronics, and lighting. You could say, however, that, with their great range and commitment to solving every customer's business challenges, they are definitely a company for the new millennium.

Founded in Germany in 1847, Siemens AG is a global leader in turning scientific innovation to practical use. Based in Munich, Germany, but with offices in and near San Jose, California,

Siemens's presence in Silicon Valley stems from Siemens AG, a 150-year-old electrical engineering and electronics company that built the first German telephone exchange.

and throughout the world, this $75 billion company has more than 450,000 employees—including 85,000 in the U.S.—and manufacturing sites in 190 countries. Yet with their focus on technological advancement, Siemens is very much a part of the entrepreneurial world.

One of the primary areas in which Siemens is working to develop new technology solutions is information and communication networks (ICNs). The Siemens company involved in this work is a leading provider of converged voice, data, and mobile communication solutions for North America. The ICN enterprise unit, located in San Jose, California, helped develop the global HiPath architecture. This architecture enables a company's existing voice and data infrastructures and applications to interoperate all over the world and over all networks. The Siemens Information and Communication Mobile (ICM) unit has invested in a wireless technology competency center in San Diego, California, which will spearhead sales, marketing, and R&D for the company's mobile phone business.

From industry-leading Fortune 500 companies to numerous government agencies, customers throughout North America rely on Siemens Business Services for complete business technology solutions. The company provides e-business expertise, management consulting, enterprise resource planning and implementation, application hosting, and operational services. Siemens also fosters innovation and entrepreneurship through its new Technology-To-Business

(TTB) Center, located in Berkeley, California. TTB, a subsidiary of Siemens Corporate Research, works to quickly convert innovative technologies into new Siemens businesses or start-ups. Working with the University of California at Berkeley and San Francisco Bay Area venture communities, TTB's vision is to combine Siemens's global reach and wide-ranging strengths with the speed and flexibility of small companies.

In the health care area, Siemens's latest innovations in cancer-fighting equipment are demonstrated in the state-of-the-art showroom at the Oncology Care Systems Group's world headquarters in Concord, California. Partnering with University of California San Francisco Health Care, Siemens has also equipped that cancer-treatment facility with its latest cancer-fighting technology. The center gives patients access to the most advanced cancer treatments and gives researchers more effective ways to continue working to beat the disease.

Siemens's energy and power unit engineers and builds fossil-fueled, hydroelectric, nuclear, and renewable-energy power plants. One of its beneficial power-distribution designs is the cogeneration plant. Here waste heat produced during power generation is captured to power nearby industries and heat nearby buildings. Three hydroelectric generators that Siemens recently rebuilt at the Grand Coulee Dam resulted in fuel cost savings of $50 million a year. Additionally, Siemens Solar is developing next-generation solar modules at its facility in Camarillo, California.

Siemens also is very involved with

Siemens Information and Communication Networks Inc. (ICN) evolved from Rolm Corporation, a Silicon Valley–based telecommunications company founded in 1969 after a court ruling allowed private equipment connections to AT&T's communications network.

semiconductors and microelectronic components. Its Infineon Technologies, which has its U.S. base in San Jose, provides semiconductor solutions for the wireless and wired communications markets, the automotive and industrial sectors, security systems, chip cards, and memory products.

With all the areas Siemens is involved in, it's not surprising that the company benefits the global community in diverse ways. One event that showcased Siemens's huge reach was the 1994 Winter Olympics in Lillehammer, Norway. There Siemens not only designed and developed the lighting, power supply, and sound systems for all the events, but also provided the transmission technology that brought the competitions to 300 million people around the world. And at the 2002 Winter Olympics, in Salt Lake City, light rail from Siemens Transportation Systems will be moving visitors from venue to venue. As Gerhard Schulmeyer, president and CEO of Siemens says, it's definitely an exciting time at Siemens.

TYCO ELECTRONICS CORPORATION

www.tycoelectronics.com

Tyco Electronics hit the ground running when it was established in September 1999. The largest unit of Tyco International, a diversified manufacturing and service company with operations in more than 100 countries, Tyco Electronics was born when Elcon Products, Silicon Valley's Raychem Corporation, and AMP were acquired and combined. Following numerous other acquisitions, Tyco Electronics is now the largest supplier of passive electronic components in the world. The corporation, based in Harrisburg, Pennsylvania, provides connectors, radar sensors, circuit protection devices, wire and cable systems, touchscreens, relays, and heat shrink products, among many others.

When Tyco Electronics acquired Raychem, the Menlo Park, California, company had been developing real-world solutions for customers since 1957. These products include systems that let telephone subscribers easily add to the number of phone lines running into their house, and point-of-sale touchscreen terminals that let waiters quickly transmit food orders to their kitchen. The company also develops arresters that help protect electrical power distribution lines from the dangers of power surges, and resettable fuses that protect cellular phones from short circuits. In addition Raychem manufactures electronic wire harnessing systems that are used in the control of planes, trains, and automobiles.

The Raychem Circuit Protection Group pioneered the advanced technology that is key to its resettable fuses. These fuses keep current flow in electronic devices from reaching dangerously high levels during fault conditions. Once the fault conditions are cleared, the fuses automatically reset themselves. Raychem's SiBar surge protectors keep sensitive telecommunications and computer-telephone equipment safe from spikes in voltage caused by lightning or power induction. The company's power switches provide protection from the effects of overly high current in universal serial port hubs and peripherals.

Another, fast-growing area in which Raychem is a leading provider is the field of fiber optics. Fiber-optic technology enables data to be transmitted via lasers over cable constructed from thin fibers of glass. Raychem has helped to make Tyco Electronics the number one supplier of fiber-optic connectors and interconnection devices, including cable assemblies, fiber management systems, and active and passive opto-electronic components. These products can be found in networks, in-flight entertainment systems, computer data centers, and the navigation systems of cars and trucks.

Along with other business units of Tyco Electronics, Raychem also contributes in a major way to the advancement of communications equipment. Raychem supplies high-demand interconnection technology for such devices as cellular phones and base stations as well as for networking hardware and transmission equipment.

Tyco Electronics is now the world's largest supplier of passive electronic components.

The company also provides high-level analysis and simulation services that enable manufacturers to predict how their systems will perform. These services result in faster design cycles and lower costs for customers. Tyco Electronics' Early Involvement Programs enable Raychem and other units to design next-generation connectors that will support communications equipment requiring more speed, higher density, and lower costs.

Computer and consumer electronics is still another area in which Raychem and other Tyco Electronics business units are producing solutions to rapidly growing global demands. Their interconnection products, including video and audio relays and input/output connectors, are key to notebook and desktop computers, engineering workstations, servers, disk drives, and business and consumer equipment.

In the automotive world, Tyco Electronics' Raychem, AMP, and M/A-COM products are used in advanced safety systems, engine controls, and power-management systems. Products including copper and fiber-optic connectors, sealing gels, "intelligent" fuses, cruise control components, sensors, and relays protect drivers and passengers and enhance the driving experience.

Though a young company in a fast-changing world, Tyco Electronics has already made its mark in a large number of markets. The company has quickly leveraged the expertise and experience of Raychem and its other business units to provide its customers with leading-edge passive electronic, wireless, and fiber-optic components. The company is also making it possible for customers to enjoy shorter lead times, faster time to market, greater economy, and a wider product line. As President Jurgen Gromer states, Tyco Electronics is ready to grow with and shape the 21st century.

INFRASTRUCTURE

SERVICE AND SUPPORT: THE SILICON VALLEY INFRASTRUCTURE

When we think of Silicon Valley today, what generally comes to mind is the sprawling area of gleaming high-tech buildings that dot the region from San Jose north and east along the bay to San Francisco. Here, in corporate headquarters and state-of-the-art research and manufacturing facilities, the wonders of the electronic world, which later appear in our schools, offices, and homes, are dreamed of, designed, and developed. Computers have grown up here, as has the Internet—in fact, some now call the area Internet Valley. We think of this region as a place where engineers, scientists, and researchers are drawn to devise the next great technologies that will be taking us further into the 21st century.

All of these things about Silicon Valley are true. The area does attract some of the brightest, most inventive members of the scientific and engineering communities. Since 1891, when former California governor Leland Stanford established Stanford University, the area that is now known as Silicon Valley has been a magnet for men and women with a thirst for scientific knowledge and the ability to put that knowledge to work for the betterment of us all.

But in addition to engineers, researchers, and university professors who teach the sciences, Silicon Valley has traditionally drawn a wide range of other highly talented people who have played key roles in enabling the region to reach the world-renowned position it now holds. These are the people and the enterprises that support the area's contribution to technological advancement by creating the dynamic infrastructure that makes it all work.

Now known for its semiconductors and Internet expertise, at the turn of the 20th century Silicon Valley was known for its fertile soil and apricot and plum orchards. The Santa Clara Valley, where much of Silicon Valley lies, was called "The Valley of Heart's Delight" for its enviable produce and temperate climate. The land occupied by the town of Palo Alto, which grew along with Stanford and from which radiated much of today's electronics industry, was mainly hayfields until 1890. But the agricultural nature of the area began to change irretrievably as Stanford became a center of scientific and engineering excellence and as it developed relationships with local businesses in which its students could pursue, in the words of Leland Stanford, "direct usefulness in life."

How did this transformation take place? How did the area change its essence from farming community to high-tech mecca?

Much of the locality's reinvention resulted from the significant appeal of living there, from the Mediterranean-like scenery to the comfortable climate to promising educational opportunities to the energy and drive of Forty-Niner descendants. In the 1970s, a *Fortune Magazine* article stated that industry shapers chose the Santa Clara Valley for their technology operations because of "A beautiful landscape of hills and plains...where fruit trees and wild flowers bloom even in February. No sooty smokestacks or shabby old factories mar the scenery." But in addition to the life style benefits, many feel that the present-day focus of Silicon Valley resulted in good part from the efforts and interests of a few key people who lived there.

One of the first people who became a force behind the telecommunications

Lee de Forest's audion tube

A typical process for an entrepreneur that comes in with an idea is that we first try to understand the idea from an intellectual property viewpoint... Then you get into really trying to help them get funded... Assuming that they get that investment, then you put a team together, starting with a board of directors, the management team, the employee base. Then the company starts to grow...We get involved with relationships internally, employees, officers, directors, management, and externally with financing, relationships with banks, leasing companies, relationships with distributors, vendors, and suppliers. A network starts to build. The enterprise really now starts to take on its own identity, its own momentum... Ultimately, perhaps, there's a public offering. Then it makes a transition from private to public enterprise, a very important transition and one that's very complex. The dynamics change now... If it's able to keep going, it may start to diversify. It does acquisitions, it establishes itself globally. Before you know it, over a period of 10 years, you can have an enterprise that employs 10,000 people, has a market value of several billions of dollars, and has gone through successions of management. We get involved in all of that. It's a very exciting thing to see it happen.

Larry Sonsini, Chairman of Wilson Sonsini Goodrich & Rosati

movement in Silicon Valley was inspired by the Morse code transmissions of Guglielmo Marconi. Douglas Perham of Palo Alto built a radio spark transmitter in the town in 1906, and was soon followed by Cyril Elwell, a Stanford engineering graduate who worked to improve on Marconi's transmitting system. To test and support his ideas, Elwell erected two 75-foot wooden antenna masts and turned his bungalow into a wireless telephone

This valley has always been fertile. I mean, they grew wheat here before the turn of the 19th century and then they started to plant fruit trees so they could promote migration from the Midwest, so people would come out and build homes. Now we've done the same thing with the sand. We've turned it into silicon.

Chuck Geschke, Founder of Adobe Systems

station. Elwell later bought Douglas Perham's house and shop and, through further invention and additional construction, turned the shop into the Federal Telegraph Company. Skilled workers eventually built 16 high-power wireless stations that formed a communications network across the country.

In 1931, the manufacturing operations of Federal Telegraph, which had grown significantly since its

You had this beautiful valley, where there was enough land for the [technology companies] to expand and grow. You had Stanford, you had Cal, you had San Francisco, then Palo Alto (which has become the financial area of the peninsula, with all the venture capitalists), and then of course you had all these people who wanted to live in California because we have this glorious world to live in, even though everybody says, gee, you're fighting the traffic, and you have this, that, and whatever. People want to be here because of the energy, because of the risk taking, because of the innovation, because of the ability to start something from nothing and create something wonderful.

Carole Rodoni, Former President and COO of Alain Pinel Realtors

A horse-drawn tiller (circa 1903) in the Santa Clara Valley

inception, were moved to New Jersey, because the local area did not yet provide all the needed suppliers and a large enough skilled labor pool. But while he was receiving his education at Stanford, a young man named Fred Terman worked briefly at Federal Telegraph. Years later, Terman was to become a key figure in both the recruitment of talented people of many backgrounds to this part of California and in the development of Silicon Valley itself.

At the close of World War II, in 1946, Terman returned to Stanford as the school's dean of engineering, certain that electronics would shortly become critical to much of everyday life. Soon after Terman took on his new role, Stanford received a contract from the U. S. Office of Naval Research, enabling the dean to set into motion several key research studies. One of these projects led to the creation of the Stanford Electronics Research Laboratories, and later to the development of the Stanford Linear Accelerator Center.

Through the end of the forties, and with Terman's ongoing efforts, government monies and bright minds continued to find their way to Stanford. Many of the skilled workers and support personnel who had been part of the area's war effort also remained. But often, after their studies were completed, many engineering graduates headed to the East Coast to secure employment. Fred Terman began to look for a way to help his bright, inventive students to stay in the area while at the same time bringing needed income to Stanford. Terman conceived of establishing a light-industrial park on leased Stanford land whose tenants would all be technology companies—companies that would work cooperatively with Stanford in line

Inside Silicon Valley's first high-tech start-up: Federal Telegraph Company (circa 1924)

with the university's purposes and research. The Stanford Industrial Park was born, and became the jumping-off point for the explosion of high-technology enterprises in the area.

The first company to build in the park, opening its doors in 1953, was Varian, whose klystron tube became the foundation of radar and microwave communication. Varian was quickly followed by Eastman Kodak, and later Hewlett-Packard, Lockheed, and General Electric. Company after company was recruited to locate in the growing technology center that was changing the landscape from hay-filled countryside to a campus of modern structures designed by world-class architects.

To make the transformation, materials suppliers, construction personnel, contractors, architects, and other building experts were needed on a continuing and large-scale basis. Companies that had started modestly in small offices—in Hewlett-Packard's case, a garage workshop—but were gaining success rapidly were ready to put up large corporate headquarters to house and make comfortable their growing numbers. The Varian brothers, for example, wanted to "accommodate the associates in a superb space that would be conducive to creative work." Special equipment also needed to be designed and produced to enable continuing research and for the companies' new products to be manufactured for their

Signetics, an integrated circuits manufacturer acquired by Philips Semiconductors in 1993

Senator Leland Stanford

waiting customers.

As the sixties unfolded, and more and more high-tech start-ups put down roots, development and building of their corporate homes continued. Many professionals eagerly came to join the exciting ventures headed by such high-tech luminaries as Robert Noyce and Andrew Grove. Now Silicon Valley began to spread south as some companies moved their semiconductor production facilities to Mountain View, Sunnyvale, Santa Clara, and San Jose, and others without Stanford ties chose to locate their headquarters further afield. Building companies also began to specialize in providing development expertise particularly for the high-tech industry, offering services to meet the unique needs for quality and construction that these electronics companies required.

In the seventies and eighties, Silicon Valley became home to additional businesses that focused on consumer electronics, microprocessors, minicomputers, software, biotechnology, and networking. Building construction and renovation continued, and now support firms provided needed services for high-tech personnel in their home lives as well as on the job. Realtors helped newly located employees and their families negotiate the often-complicated process of finding a place to call home. Banks invested in and supported business development and the growth of communities. Amusement parks and other recreational facilities were created to provide sources of fun for leisure hours.

Opposite page: Robert Noyce receiving National Medal of Technology from Ronald Reagan, 1987

New businesses sprang up to offer a wide variety of goods and services to the growing population.

With the nineties came handheld electronic devices, the growth of the Internet, and advancements in numerous technologies—and the companies that moved them forward. Momentum in design and manufacturing processes made many new products available, as did the services of legal firms that provided the expertise needed to bring start-ups public and protect their intellectual property rights. Many companies, including those that offered accounting, building maintenance, marketing communications, financial, employment, and fabrication services, continued to focus on the special support needs of the high-tech community.

While continually drawing talented scientists and engineers from all parts of the world, Silicon Valley has also been lucky to attract the crucial service providers who help to turn concepts into realities and who support daily life in this dynamic area. With their skills, knowledge, and diversity, they ensure that the "Valley of Heart's Delight" remains a premier place to work and live.

Robert Noyce at the podium, stockholders' meeting, 1979

Mackay Radio

By 1908, Cyril Elwell was convinced that only continuous-wave radio was commercially feasible. He sailed to Denmark and licensed the rights to Danish scientist Valdemar Poulsen's arc converter, which could produce continuous waves. On his return, Elwell struck out in his attempt to raise capital in New York City, where promoters had given wireless radio a bad name. Back in Palo Alto, Stanford President David Starr Jordan offered to invest $500. With Jordan's and other Stanford University professors' financial backing, the Poulsen Wireless Telephone and Telegraph Company was born and became Silicon Valley's first high-technology start-up.

Cyril Elwell, Stanford University varsity track team member, founded the Poulsen Wireless Telephone and Telegraph Company in 1909. Later the company was re-named the Federal Telegraph Company.

Lee de Forest inspecting an early audion tube

Cyril Elwell (far left) and Lee de Forest (center)

THERMA, INC.

www.therma.com

Be creative. Be adaptable. Take risks—and have fun while you're doing it. If you asked Joe Parisi, president of Therma, Inc., how he and his company became so successful—and how you can become successful too—that's most likely what he would tell you. The formula certainly worked for Parisi and his wife, Nicki, who is Therma's co-founder and its chief financial officer. Therma, Inc. is currently the largest mechanical contracting services company in Silicon Valley's Santa Clara County, and its employees have worked on more electronics, biotechnology, and semiconductor plants than any other mechanical contractor in the area.

The Parisis and their young company needed to be creative, flexible risk takers right from the moment they went into business in San Jose, California, in 1967. Their first customers were the equally young high-tech companies that were beginning to populate the valley—companies that needed a wide variety of building services as they set up their offices and manufacturing plants. Though Therma specialized in mechanical contracting—providing air conditioning systems, piping, plumbing, refrigeration, cleanrooms, and exhaust systems—they took on and saw through just about any job they could to make ends meet. They acted as electrical contractors, sprinkler contractors, even delivered parts to maintenance crews. Whatever a client needed in order to make their business operational, Therma said yes and found a way to do it for them.

Their creativity, flexibility, and persistence paid off. The company quickly established a reputation for reliability and ingenuity, and the staff

President Clinton visits the Therma facilities on May 1, 1998

worked hard to establish personal relationships with all of their clients. As the electronics industry took off, the emerging leaders thought of Therma, and called on the firm for help with their expanding facilities needs. Because the industry was so new, Therma ended up designing and then custom-making much of the special equipment the fledgling companies needed, including acid neutralization systems, double-contained pipes to move exotic gases, and fume scrubbers. They even made chemical sinks for a while because there just weren't many companies making the kinds of devices the semiconductor industry needed. But Therma was willing and able. The staff designed the first fabrication plants for Advanced Micro Devices, helped Fairchild solve a problem with a diffusion furnace, and laid piping for Intel's original offices.

Because they were so willing to innovate and adapt, Therma was able to grow right along with their customers. Following the team approach, their engineers, designers, systems analysts, and fabricators not only interacted with each other to find solutions to new challenges, but also worked directly with their clients and their clients' architects and designers. This open, creative environment helped Therma produce more efficient, higher-performing mechanical systems and to pioneer new methods for controlling critical processing elements, such as heat, humidity, and hazardous waste. They designed the first large air conditioning system that had variable-speed motors to conserve energy and reduce costs. They designed tables for Stanford University Medical School that vented formaldehyde fumes—solving a problem that had been troubling medical students for years. And they also developed numerous products that have become industry standards, such as portable cleanrooms for semiconductor fabrication.

In addition to designing essential mechanical systems, Therma also fabricates much of those systems' parts. Their brand-new 300,000-square-foot facility in San Jose houses one of the premier metal shops in Northern California, where skilled employees manufacture everything from ductwork to piping to utility skids. The company was one of the first fully computerized mechanical contractors in the industry, and continues to use the latest technology and the best tools to produce state-of-the-art systems. The spotless shop was designed to be a safe, comfortable place for employees to work.

Therma's beautiful theme-oriented cafeteria

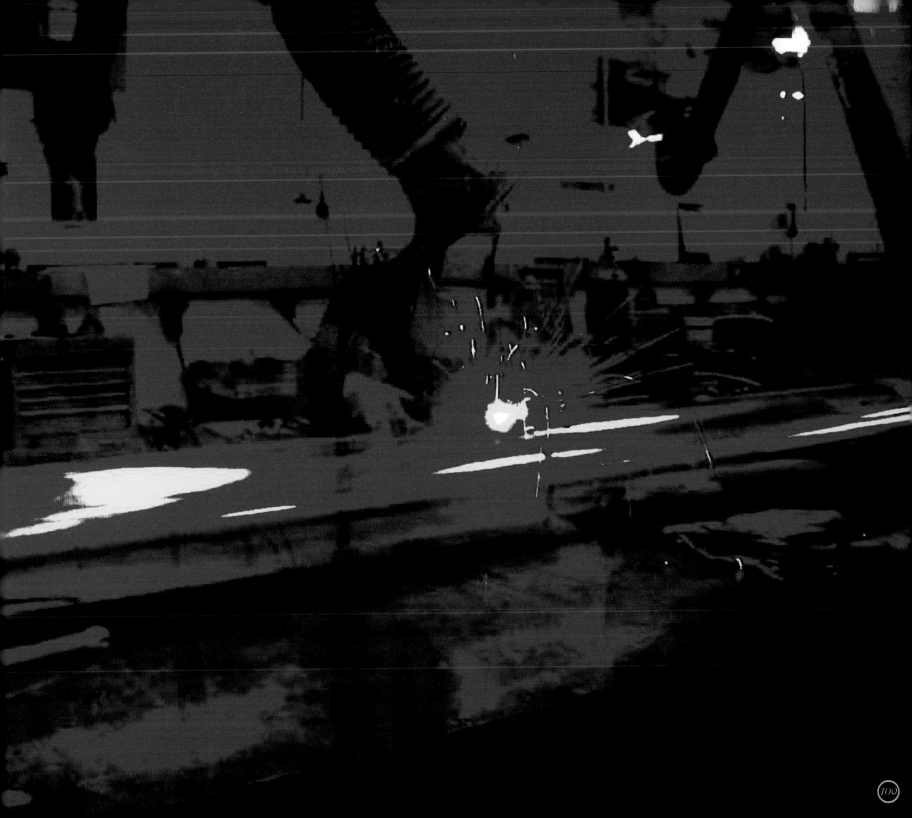

After systems have been designed and constructed, Therma's plumbers, steamfitters, and mechanics see to their installation. But their service doesn't stop there. Once a system is operating smoothly, mechanics make sure that it continues to do so by providing a customized maintenance program. Therma-owned service vans and their satellite tracking system enable a fast response to any customer's needs. Employees also are quick to help clients during emergencies; following the Loma Prieta earthquake of 1989, Therma workers put in thousands of hours of overtime to restore customers' piping and mechanical systems.

Because Therma's owners and employees have been so willing to adapt and innovate and "think outside the box," a wide range of people and businesses have sought them out to solve mechanical engineering problems. No job is ever too big or too small—a project might bring in revenues of $100 or many millions of dollars, but each is a challenge that brings an energetic response. Recently a company that invented a thermal photography technique that can detect breast cancer up to nine years before it might otherwise be discovered came to the Parisis to devise a way to house and transport the apparatus. Therma engineers developed a cleanroom trailer with a temperature- and humidity-controlled environment in which the equipment can be safely used, stored, and conveyed to remote locations. A prototype container was built on the premises, and many more will now be

Large pipe being fashioned at the Therma facility located at 1601 Las Plumas Avenue in San Jose, California

built and equipped, then put to work for critical cancer detection throughout the country.

Along with adaptability, innovation, and serving their customers well, the Parisis believe there is another key to their success—serving their employees well. The couple has always felt great gratitude to their staff, and touts them as the best in the business. Employees are given decision-making capabilities and are encouraged to contribute to every process. They are also encouraged to take on charitable work—Therma will often donate financially to worthy causes and employees will donate their time. To thank their employees, and to enrich and expand their lives, Therma provides them with an art-filled facility, which includes an enormous replica of Michelangelo's David as well as high-tech furniture and

artwork made with cutting-edge technology on Therma's site. The large and bright lunchroom is painted with European landscapes and street scenes, a spot where workers can relax and recharge in the middle of their busy day.

Precision welding is a highly specialized and critical skill set of Therma's engineering team.

While most of their work has been done within Silicon Valley, Therma has also helped to set up the first semiconductor plant in China and has contributed to projects in other parts of Asia as well as throughout Europe. Their unwillingness to be limited in their scope has also evolved into ever increasing amounts of work in the biotech arena, an industry that is still so new that many companies that receive funding don't know how to set up labs or meet government regulations. While the technology is different, Therma's expertise with the mechanical systems needed for semiconductor manufacturing carries over into the biotech world, and, as always, Therma's engineers share their knowledge. The company is also becoming more involved with designing and installing systems needed in data centers, where large numbers of computers must be housed securely so that their data is always accessible. Such centers often require dual mechanical systems to assure that the computers are never down.

As it always has, Therma and its employees are working to meet not only immediate mechanical system challenges but clients' future needs as well. With this goal in mind, they are usually the first to try new equipment and technology, and find that their risk taking generally pays off; their current use of lasers for metal cutting enables them to do things that other fabricators cannot. For Therma, being open to change while providing the best service possible is the only way of life.

Robotic laser cutters are just one of the highly advanced types of equipment in use at Therma.

BANK OF AMERICA

www.bankofamerica.com

Bank of America is aptly named. Not only is it the largest American bank, but it is also the remarkable realization of the ambitions, innovations, and accomplishments of more than 2,000 predecessor banks across the country.

Farmers Bank of Maryland was at the start of it all. Created in 1805 to serve local farmers, rather than the wealthy, the forward-thinking bank became the first bank in the country to pay interest on deposits. Another bank that would become part of what eventually became Bank of America was Boatmen's Bank, founded in St. Louis to offer banking to boatmen who worked along the Mississippi. In Seattle, the store that eventually would become the Seattle First National Bank, or Seafirst, provided a place where mill hands, trappers, and miners could safely keep their money. In Chicago, business and political leaders joined forces to open a community bank they called Merchants Savings. And in North Carolina, two banks key to today's Bank of America sprang up: American Trust, founded on the principles of personal responsibility, private enterprise, and ingenuity; and North Carolina National Bank, whose early motto was "Ask those we serve."

Meanwhile, in San Francisco, A.P. Giannini, the son of Italian immigrants, opened the Bank of Italy in 1904 to bring "banking to the little guy" by meeting the financial needs of the many immigrants who were moving to the American West. Giannini, or A.P., as he was known to all, became a key player in the development of California. On a handshake, A.P. provided loans to finance the rebuilding of San Francisco after the 1906 earthquake, pioneered the concept of statewide branch banking, underwrote the financing of the Golden Gate Bridge and other infrastructure projects, developed banking services for women, and financed the fledgling film industry. By 1930 the Bank of Italy was the largest statewide banking system in the country, and Giannini changed its name to Bank of America to reflect his vision of growth and his ambitions for nationwide banking.

As Bank of America continued to innovate and expand, so too did North Carolina National Bank. Following its goal to provide hometown banking through local people concerned for their community's economic and civic development, NCNB exploited opportunities in interstate banking regulations to expand into other southern states and then merged with C&S/Sovran Corporation. To reflect the new bank's vision of service and growth, the company was renamed NationsBank in 1992 and quickly acquired Barnett Banks in Florida to make it the dominant banking force in the South.

In 1998, southern powerhouse NationsBank merged with West Coast powerhouse Bank of America to realize both banks' visions and to create a nationwide network of enterprise and ingenuity. The new Bank of America became the nation's largest bank, with over 4,500 banking centers, 14,000 ATM machines, 30 million customers, and banking activities in 190 countries.

As it grew and brought much needed banking services to both "little people" and businesses around the globe, Bank of America made major contributions to the advancement of the banking industry. During Franklin Roosevelt's administration, Boatmen's Bank pioneered the insuring of deposits through the Federal Deposit Insurance Corporation. Bank of America also put early computer technology to work by partnering with the Stanford Research Institute to create ERMA, the Electronic Recording Method of Accounting. ERMA, for the first time, enabled checks to be processed automatically by incorporating Magnetic Ink Character Recognition, or MICR, the computer encoding of checks that revolutionized banking.

Bank of America put its employees' ingenuity to work to develop other technology-based innovations. It created Bankamericard, which became Visa, the most widely accepted credit card in the world. It also introduced the first 24-hour ATM machines. Today, Bank of America continues to innovate with Web-based ATMs, sophisticated online banking, and a fingerprint-based system that provides access to online banking with the security features of the SmartCard.

For nearly 200 years, Bank of America has had a profound interest in serving both people and their communities. This commitment can be seen today in the billions of dollars as well as the many volunteer hours the company has pledged to a wide array of housing, community-development, and educational efforts. Bank of America's heritage of ingenuity and innovation continues to produce exciting technological and service innovations for customers and business clients across America and around the world.

PACIFIC MAINTENANCE

www.pmc-ibm.com

In Silicon Valley, as in other areas that are home to semiconductor, biotechnology, pharmaceutical, or aerospace companies, building maintenance doesn't consist only of keeping windows sparkling and carpets dirt free, as important as those services are. When chemicals, bacteria, or environmental pollutants are part of a fabrication or biomedical process, a full-spectrum service program is needed to keep facilities clean—and workers and surrounding communities safe from hazardous materials as well.

Pacific Maintenance Company provides a complete range of commercial custodial services. Though it began in 1931 maintaining offices and providing window-cleaning services, the company now specializes in working with the technical and biomedical industries' unique cleaning needs. With over 1,400 cleaning professionals servicing

Ultra-contamination-free "cleanrooms." Specialty cleaning for microcontamination control.

more than 25 million feet of factories and offices each night, Pacific Maintenance plays an important part in the health and safety of the high-tech world.

Electrostatic discharge, or ESD, is a particular problem for technology manufacturing companies—to the tune of an estimated $15 billion in damages, lost data, and warranty claims per year. When dissimilar materials are separated, an electrical charge can be generated—one that can destroy computer data, memory circuits, components, and manufactured products. Pacific Maintenance offers a full range of ESD-containment services, including dust-free dry polishing and non-skid ESD floor finishes.

Another area in which Pacific Maintenance specializes is micro-contamination control. As more and more circuits are being packed onto wafers, ultra-contamination-free "cleanrooms" are needed to process them defect free. Pacific Maintenance works with customers to provide programs to suit their specific needs, including determining goals, arranging for specialty cleaning work, such as cleaning needed in class 1 environments and aseptic areas, and measuring results, for example, counting particles and taking ESD readings. As with all the work they do, safety, for both employees and clients, is utmost.

George Hernandez, president of Pacific Maintenance Company, is proud that his company services "some of the cleanest buildings in the world." His home office in Santa Clara, California, and the nine additional company offices located throughout the western United States, may soon be joined by an office on the East Coast.

1931–1956 Pacifico Chioini, president and founder

1956–1980 Giulio Chioini, president

1980–1991 John Cruz, president

1991– George Hernandez, president

PRICEWATERHOUSE-COOPERS LLP

www.pwcglobal.com

To succeed in today's highly competitive marketplace, technology companies need to do more than design, manufacture, and distribute products. They need to have in place the complex business systems—from finance to tax management to operations—that allow them to operate successfully. Drawing on the knowledge and skills of 155,000 people in 150 countries, PricewaterhouseCoopers helps technology clients, from start-ups to global giants, meet a full range of business needs, including audit, assurance, business advisory, financial advisory, and global tax.

PricewaterhouseCoopers LLP is located in the heart of Silicon Valley.

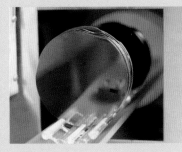

From finance to tax management to operations, PricewaterhouseCoopers provides technology clients with business support.

PricewaterhouseCoopers' Global Technology Industry Group, led by Paul Weaver, is comprised of partners in all high-growth technology markets around the world. Based in the heart of Silicon Valley, it serves numerous sectors: the Internet, software, computers and

PricewaterhouseCoopers is involved in all areas of high-growth technology markets.

networking, semiconductors, life sciences, and venture capital. This global team has been recognized for guiding more venture capital–backed companies through the IPO process than any other professional services firm. The Group also sponsors the Money Tree™ Survey, a quarterly report tracking investments in private U.S. companies made by venture capitalists. In addition it sponsors the VC BestPractices™ Series. All of the Group's technology-industry survey reports, advisories, and sector-specific articles can be linked to through the company's Web site.

PricewaterhouseCoopers' Silicon Valley office is located at 10 Almaden Boulevard, San Jose, California.

PricewaterhouseCoopers' Venture Capital Group is another important part of the company. Led by Tracy Lefteroff, it is the first choice among the top venture capital and private equity firms throughout the United States for both tax consulting and accounting services. This group has been selected as tax advisors and auditors by more venture capital firms than any other provider.

TOENISKOETTER & BREEDING, INC.

www.tbionline.com

When they founded their construction and development companies in 1983, Chuck Toeniskoetter and Dan Breeding worried that the name Toeniskoetter & Breeding would be too difficult for people to remember. They need not have been concerned. By the end of the 1990s, their San Jose, California–based Toeniskoetter & Breeding, Inc. Construction had completed more than $450 million in projects, and Toeniskoetter & Breeding, Inc. Development had completed more

*Integrated Circuit Systems,
525 Race Street, San Jose, California*

than 1.5 million square feet of building space with an equal amount under development. The company's third arm, Toeniskoetter & Breeding Property Management, was managing more than 1 million square feet of commercial real estate. In fact, by the end of the century, Toeniskoetter & Breeding, Inc. (TBI) was one of Silicon Valley's fastest growing privately held companies,

and the two founders were named "1999 Real Estate Entrepreneurs of the Year" by the *San Jose/Silicon Valley Business Journal*.

TBI Construction started out by focusing on building interiors, with much of its initial work in the health care industry. In today's market, interiors are still a bigger business than building shells, and TBI is the acknowledged leader in high-end professional offices and corporate headquarters. The company has built professional offices for law firms, accounting firms, venture capitalists, and investment bankers. It has also built company headquarters for Hewlett-Packard, Agilent Technologies, Silicon Valley Bank, Amdahl, Knight Ridder, CS First Boston, and Comerica Bank, among many others.

Toeniskoetter & Breeding is also the acknowledged leader in historical building restoration. Among its achievements are the restoration and seismic strengthening of a number of San Jose–area facilities: the 106-year-old St. Joseph's Cathedral, the 124-year-old Santa Clara County Courthouse, the 90-year-old Sacred Heart Church, and the San Jose Unified School District's Hoover School. The company also specializes in remodeling and additions to educational facilities, including eight schools in the Santa Clara Unified School District, Archbishop Mitty High School in San Jose, and San Jose State University's business school. TBI also built St. Francis of Assisi Church in San Jose and a new structure for Shir Hadash in Los Gatos, and remodeled Congregation Beth Am in Palo Alto. In

addition the firm has built R&D facilities for SDL, Sun Microsystems, Dionex Corp., and Hewlett-Packard.

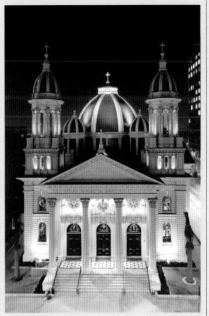

*St. Joseph's Cathedral,
San Jose, California*

One of the reasons for Toeniskoetter & Breeding's success in the public sector is the development and employment of its Multiple Prime Construction Management Program. Using this program, TBI serves as both construction manager and owner's agent. Staff members take active roles in the design process, produce reliable budgets and schedules, and represent their client when contracting with subcontractors.

TBI's work on the recent Agilent Technologies project in Palo Alto illustrates the degree to which TBI has adopted technology to improve construction practices. Company employees used e-mail to obtain building

permits; speed communication with architects, clients, and vendors; and send blueprints and spreadsheets. Agilent employees were able to follow the progress of construction through a Web site with continuous video broadcasting.

As part of its business, TBI Construction constructs new buildings for Toeniskoetter & Breeding, Inc. Development. TBI Development, managed since its inception by President Brad Krouskup, has developed more than 1.5 million square feet of office, retail, medical office, and industrial properties. One million square feet have remained in the TBI portfolio.

TBI Development also serves as managing general partner for a number of diversified real estate properties throughout California's Santa Clara and Santa Cruz counties. These properties include the 110-acre Madrone Business Park and the 30-acre Cochrane Business Ranch in Morgan Hill; 450 West Santa Clara Street, the O'Connor Health Center, and the western headquarters for Integrated Circuit Systems, all in San Jose; Gateway Square in Campbell; and Granite Creek Business Center in Scotts Valley.

Much of Toeniskoetter & Breeding's success can be attributed to its ability to form successful partnerships—with landowners, with investors, and with businesses seeking equity in the facilities they occupy. The most important and enduring partnership, however, remains between the founders, whose names are not only remembered, but are synonymous with building excellence.

WILSON SONSINI GOODRICH & ROSATI

www.wsgr.com

When the three-attorney law firm that would become Wilson Sonsini Goodrich & Rosati (WSGR) first hung out its shingle in Palo Alto, California, very few local law firms were handling business law. There were also very few technology companies populating what is now Silicon Valley. In a completely real sense, high tech and WSGR have come of age together, by driving and supporting each other's growth.

Now more than 800 lawyers strong, Wilson Sonsini Goodrich & Rosati is the largest law firm in California, and is known as the top counsel to the high-tech industry. Clients of the firm include Sun, 3Com, Inktomi, C/NET, Garage.com, and Hewlett-Packard, to name just a few. And the services WSGR provides take its clients from start-up to initial public offering to the Fortune 500.

Larry Sonsini, one of the firm's founders and its current chairman, believes that WSGR's growth and reputation are the result of its goal of being a strategic business partner to its clients. The law firm works to assist companies at every stage of their development—not just to handle one particular legal function. "We do whatever it takes to serve the client," Sonsini says. That includes supporting and advising companies on public offerings, or selling stock in the company to shareholders; financing;

From left to right: Partners John Wilson, Larry Sonsini, Mario Rosati, and John Goodrich

restructuring; international transactions; intellectual property issues; employment relationships; mergers; taxes; criminal defense; and trademarking.

While WSGR does represent clients in the financial, health, life sciences, and consumer products fields, it is best known for its work with technology companies. This focus comes from the firm's headquarters location in Silicon Valley. It also comes from WSGR's mission to support such companies as they drive innovation and benefit people in their home, school, and business lives.

One area in which the law firm works closely with technology companies is in intellectual property management, or the protection of a business's ideas. Such ideas, while not tangible, are often critical to a company's survival and growth. In fact, a start-up company's idea may be its only real asset. WSGR's Strategic Intellectual Property

Representation helps to shelter these valuable assets by providing legal assistance in many ways. These include identifying inventions to protect, targeting particular technologies to license or buy, enforcing clients' intellectual property rights, and preventing clients from treading on competitors' rights.

Another area in which WSGR's expertise supports technology and other businesses is in corporate and securities law. The firm's attorneys counsel clients in obtaining financing, from finding seed money to "going public." They also work to negotiate mergers, prevent hostile takeovers, and set up joint ventures. Presently they advise more than 300 public and 3,000 private companies.

Employment law is another practice on which WSGR focuses. The attorneys provide advice and counsel on every area of the employer/employee relationship, from hiring to firing to discrimination to workplace harassment. They also represent clients, both individuals and corporations, in criminal cases. As part of this work they handle investigations, grand jury inquiries, and trials.

Because the firm doesn't restrict itself to working with only well-established firms, business people just starting out can benefit from WSGR's counsel. In fact, entrepreneurs can find many helpful resources through the firm's Web site before they even become a client. Information on the site includes a sample business plan, insight into what funding organizations look for when they

consider an investment, sources to learn about employee benefits, and how to reach an online portal that focuses exclusively on legal matters. The law firm also provides service without charge to a number of organizations that need access to the legal system but don't have the funds to do so. These groups include the AIDS Legal Referral Panel and the Legal Advocates for Children

WSGR is headquartered in Palo Alto, California.

and Youth Guardianship Project.

Because of its close ties to the technology industry, WSGR recently opened three new offices in the high tech–heavy areas of Kirkland, Washington; Austin, Texas; and McLean, Virginia. And because of these ties, the firm is now deeply involved with the new body of law that is developing around issues concerning the Internet. These issues include access, taxation, and regulation, among others, and will command growing attention as the law firm continues to support and represent its technology clients.

KEEBLE AND SHUCHAT

www.kspphoto.com

Terry Shuchat, owner of photographic-equipment store Keeble and Shuchat, grew up with Silicon Valley. He started working at a Palo Alto, California, camera store after school when he was just in the ninth grade—a time when Stanford University, not yet electronics, put the small town on the map—and opened Keeble and Shuchat in 1965. As the electronics industry grew and became a force in the area, so too did Keeble and Shuchat grow and evolve—from a small business that provided commercial photography services to the company that today supplies state-of-the-art cameras and photographic equipment to technology giants and start-ups alike.

In 1965, Keeble and Shuchat had a 1,000-square-foot facility and a great reputation as a commercial photography studio. The company also had a great location, and began to work with some of the electronics firms that had started to populate the area. In the mid-'60s, when Hewlett-Packard was just introducing its first computer, Keeble and Shuchat was processing the film taken by HP's Palo Alto–based photographer. As time went on, and their relationships with local companies developed, they began to see that tech companies needed the newest photographic and filming equipment as well as commercial photography services. They added a small camera store to the business, and began their transformation. Today, Keeble and Shuchat no longer

Keeble and Shuchat Photography, one of the company's two professional photography locations in Palo Alto, California

provides commercial photography, but instead fills two buildings, a total of 25,000 square feet, with the most advanced photo and filming equipment around.

Though they sell to advanced amateur and professional photographers, and provide photofinishing and other services, a large part of their business continues to be with Silicon Valley electronics firms. Many of these companies have established their own on-site studios to more easily take care of their imaging and recording needs—for presentations, workshops, training, demonstrations, and the like. Representatives from Keeble and Shuchat work with these companies' staffs to set up and equip their studios with the best solutions possible. They recommend and integrate lighting, digital cameras, electronic studios, and filming equipment. They also provide darkroom supplies and slides, and a wide range of professional equipment to rent.

As it has grown, a priority for the company has been to keep a strong connection with each customer. Staff members are continually trained in the latest equipment and techniques, so they can provide up-to-the-minute information to both experienced professionals and newcomers to the field alike. Terry Shuchat feels that the company's longevity is due to this extensive training and to developing personal relationships with clients—he notes that corporate founders, CEOs, as well as employees and their families all shop at the store. He also notes that, just as Keeble and Shuchat has already come a long way with the electronics industry, he intends that it will continue to grow as electronics reach greater and greater heights.

INFRASTRUCTURE

ALAIN PINEL REALTORS

www.apr.com

A compelling factor driving Alain Pinel Realtors' rapid surge to become the largest independent real estate company in the San Francisco Bay Area

was applying a major force behind the success of the region it serves—technology. The company was the first real estate business in the country to network all of its sales professionals and offices with T1 Internet access, and the first whose realtors use e-mail to communicate with each other and their clients. It was also the first realty company in the U.S. to put up a Web site and the first to provide an "e-mail robot" that notifies clients when a listing matching their requirements comes on the market.

Their revolutionary use of technology, combined with their marketing know-how, has quickly turned Alain Pinel Realtors into an industry leader. Launched in Saratoga, California, in August 1990, the company rang up sales of over $20,000,000 in its first four months. Just nine years later, sales volume was over $5,000,000,000, and the company now boasts 23 offices and more than 950 sales professionals. Alain Pinel Realtors has been recognized annually as one of the fastest-growing companies in Northern California.

Founder and owner Paul Hulme was certain that the traditional way of handling real estate transactions was no longer working, and that innovation, risk taking, and teamwork were needed. He understood that buying or selling a home is more than just a business transaction—it is the beginning of a new way of living, and definitely an emotional experience. He decided to offer a service that would help his clients have the smoothest, easiest, most positive experience possible.

Alain Pinel Realtors now provides every service needed for a successful home purchase or sale—from virtual home tours and instant access to listings, including prestigious Christie's Great Estates properties, to mortgage-search assistance and relocation help. The company's award-winning services focus directly on its home buyers and sellers; many of the processes are automated, and all of the business aspects can be handled right in the realtor's office. Former president and COO Carole Rodoni believes that people buying and selling homes are looking for this efficient, positive way to move through the process.

One of the reasons Alain Pinel Realtors is able to offer so many

services with such ease is its proprietary technology system, called Savi™. Savi, or Superior Access Via Internet, is a suite of Java-based applications that are available to Alain Pinel sales professionals over the company's intranet within seconds. The system searches for and broadcasts information, including maps and graphics, on all listed properties to all sales professionals immediately. It also generates comparative property and market analyses, and is linked to the company's Web site and hot-linked to Yahoo! to give listings wide exposure. Savi also automates many realty-related tasks, and makes it easy to share information with other realtors, clients, and partners, such as banks and title companies. Through the system, sales professionals have a "virtual office" at their fingertips, 24 hours a day, 7 days a week.

The company's Web site is another major factor in Alain Pinel Realtors' success. Named one of the best real estate Internet sites in the world by a noted real estate writer, the site offers a free e-mail subscription service in which clients indicate their home needs, such as number of bedrooms, then are automatically notified when a suitable house comes on the market. Visitors can also take 360-degree virtual home tours and learn more about communities or school districts they're interested in.

With its marketing, Alain Pinel Realtors makes its listings stand out by including inviting copy and lush images, and focuses on individuals and families who are looking for a particular life style and community. The company has its own in-house advertising and marketing department that develops effective sales literature and provides a timely marketing campaign for each new listing, Staff members work with both realtors and their clients to make certain that property descriptions are accurate and appealing, and reach the widest audience possible.

Like its dynamic high-tech neighbors, Alain Pinel Realtors is combining technology and expertise to bring about change, success, and growth in Silicon Valley and beyond.

Alain Pinel Realtors' Web portal located at http://www.apr.com

U.S. Navy dirigible flying over Moffett Field located in Mountain View, California, 1934.

MEMORIAL CHURCH
ERECTED TO THE GLORY OF GOD AND IN LOVING MEMORY OF MY HUSBAND LELAND STANFORD

Stanford Memorial Church after the
1906 earthquake

PHOTO CREDITS

Book cover, Santa Clara Valley, 1937, Dan Baker

Pp. 2 & 3: Stanford University Archive (hereinafter SUA)

P. 4, Holly Winslow

P. 7, Coherent, Inc.

P. 10, BL, Palo Alto Historical Association (hereinafter PAHA)

Pp. 10 & 11, Intel Corporation

P. 12, SUA

P. 13, Intel Corporation

P. 14, SUA

P. 15, Infineon Technologies (hereinafter IT)

Pp. 16 & 17, SUA

Pp. 18 & 19, NEC, C&I Photography

P. 19, LL, Rick Der

Pp. 20 & 21, C&I Photography, Samsung Semiconductor

P. 23, Linear Technology

P. 24, Cypress Semiconductor

P. 25, Asyst Technologies

Pp. 26 & 27, Vishay Intertechnology, Inc.

Pp. 28 & 29, IT

P. 30, Atmel Corporation

P. 31, Flextronics International Ltd.

P. 33, Varian Associates

P. 34, Gutenberg Museum, Mantz, Germany

P. 35, SUA

P. 36, SUA

P. 37, TL, SUA

P. 37, TR, Apple

P. 39, Apple

Pp. 40 & 41, Inktomi

P. 42, Hewlett-Packard Company

P. 43, Avaya

P. 44, Oracle Corporation

P. 45, Cisco Systems

P. 46, Adobe Systems

P. 47, Quantum Corporation

P. 48, TM, Fujitsu Software Corporation

P. 48, BM, Institute for the History of Technology

P. 49, Adaptec, Inc.

P. 50, BL, Achille Bigliardi Photography, Hitachi

P. 50, TR, Hitachi Instruments, Inc.

P. 51, TL, Hitachi Instruments, Inc.

P. 51, BR, C&I Photography

P. 52, Autodesk

P. 53, Apple

P. 54, Sound Advantage

P. 55, Trend Micro, Inc.

Pp. 56 & 57, Network Appliance

P. 58, SONICblue, Inc.

P. 60, Acuson

P. 61, Varian Associates

P. 62, Target Therapeutics

P. 63, Collagen

P. 64, Varian Associates

Pp. 66 & 67, Varian Medical Systems

P. 68, Agilent Technologies, permission of use granted

P. 69, SRI International

P. 70, Acuson

P. 71, Coherent, Inc.

P. 72, courtesy of IBM, unauthorized use not permitted

P. 73, PAHA

P. 74, BL, courtesy of IBM, unauthorized use not permitted

P. 74, TR, Varian Associates

P. 75, Varian Associates

P. 76, BL, Allan Dean Walker

P. 76, middle, SETI

P. 76, BR, courtesy of IBM, unauthorized use not permitted

P. 77, Syntex Corporation

P. 78, SUA

P. 79, SUA

P. 80, SUA

P. 81, SUA

Pp. 82 & 83, PAHA

P. 84, SUA

P. 85, PAHA

P. 86, SUA

P. 87, SUA

P. 88, Hewlett-Packard Company

P. 89, Varian Associates

P. 90, Varian Associates

P. 91, PAHA

P. 92, Intel Corporation

P. 93, *Palo Alto Times Tribune*/Joe Melena

Pp. 94 & 95, courtesy of IBM, unauthorized use not permitted

Pp. 96 & 97, Intel Corporation

P. 98, Siemens AG

P. 99, Brad Milliken

P. 100, SUA

P. 101, PAHA

P. 102, PAHA

P. 103, LL, Philips Semiconductors

P. 103, LR, SUA

P. 104, Intel Corporation

P. 105, Intel Corporation

P. 106, SUA

P. 107, PAHA

P. 108, Therma, Inc.

P. 109, Therma, Inc.

P. 110, Therma, Inc.

P. 111, Therma, Inc.

P. 113, Pacific Maintenance

P. 114, ML, BM, PricewaterhouseCoopers

P. 114, building photos, Mats Bodin, Bodin Studio

P. 115, ML, Toeniskoetter & Breeding

P. 115, middle, Jane Lidz

P. 116, Wilson Sonsini Goodrich & Rosati

P. 117, Institute for the History of Technology

P. 118, Alain Pinel Realtors

P. 119, Moffett Field Historical Museum

P. 120, *Palo Alto Times Tribune*

P. 121, PAHA

P. 122, SUA

BIBLIOGRAPHY

Altenberg, Lee, *Beyond Capitalism: Leland Stanford's Forgotten Vision*, Stanford, Stanford Historical Society, 1990.

Bunch, Bryan, and Hellemans, Alexander, *The Timetables of Science*, New York, Simon and Schuster, 1988.

Di Salvo, Chris, *San Jose & Silicon Valley: Primed for the 21st Century*, Montgomery, Ala., Community Communications, Inc., 1997.

Forester, Tom, *High-Tech Society*, Cambridge, Mass., The MIT Press, 1987.

Henderson, Judith, ed., *Reflections of the Past—An Anthology of San Jose*, Encitas, Calif., Heritage Media Corporation, 1996.

Malone, Michael S., *The Big Score: the Billion Dollar Story of Silicon Valley*, Garden City, N.Y., Doubleday & Company, 1985.

Morgan, Jane, *Electronics in the West: The First 50 Years*, Palo Alto, National Press Books, 1967.

Packard, David, *The HP Way: How Bill Hewlett and I Built Our Company*, edited by David Kirby with Karen Lewis, Palo Alto, Harper Business, 1995.

Panati, Charles, *Extraordinary Origins of Everyday Things*, New York, Harper & Row, 1987.

Robertson, Douglas S., *The New Renaissance*, New York, Oxford University Press, 1998.

Sagan, Carl, *The Demon-Haunted World: Science as a Candle in the Dark*, New York, Ballantine Books, 1997.

San Jose Mercury News, various.

Santa Clara Valley Historical Association, video interviews of Silicon Valley inventors, company founders, and others, Palo Alto, 1993–2001.

Sexton, Jean Deitz, *Silicon Valley: Inventing the Future*, Windsor Publications, 1992.

van Dulken, Stephen, *Inventing the 20th Century*, New York, New York University Press, 2000.

Winslow, Ward, ed., *The Making of Silicon Valley: A 100 Year Renaissance*, Palo Alto, Santa Clara Valley Historical Association, 1995.

Winslow, Ward, *Varian: 50 Years*, Palo Alto, Santa Clara Valley Historical Association, 1998.

Winslow, Ward, and the Palo Alto Historical Association, *Palo Alto: A Centennial History*, Palo Alto, Palo Alto Historical Association, 1993.

Winters, Paul A., ed., *The Information Revolution*, San Diego, Calif., Greenhaven Press, 1998.

Web sites:
www.ocf.berkeley.edu
www.gel.usherb.ca
www.netvalley.com
www.ciol.com
www.isoc.org
www.ox.compsoc.net
www.digitalcentury.com
www.superkids.com
www.cs.colorado.edu
www.scottlan.edu
www.parc.xerox.com
www.seti.org
www.ti.com